AN UNTITLED BOOK ABOUT PARENTING.

January to March

Blake C. Aldwine

AN UNTITLED BOOK ABOUT PARENTING

PAPERBACK EDITION

ISBN 13: 978-1-906529-59-8
This book combines the two previous Kindle releases.

'An Untitled Book About Parenting. January.'
ASIN: B084VV6KDJ. ISBN-13: 9781906529352.

'An 'Extra' Untitled Book About Parenting. February & March.'
ASIN: B086QZQ5LQ. ISBN-13: 9781906529550.

Dedications

To my family.
To my friends.
To the wonderful beyond your wildest dreams.
To those who smile, laugh, tell jokes, and dance when the
rhythm gets them, even on the tough days.

To the entire world. These are fearful times.
#ClapforNHS #Clapforourcarers

Introduction

Happy New Year, everyone! It's so great to meet you all. I'm Blake Cameron Aldwine.

So, who am I? What am I? Well, I'm a fiancé, father of four, and a hardworking guy. I love to work and live in the book world. I mean, it's a magical place, pure magic. Twenty-six letters in the alphabet. Twenty-six. Try and remember all the books you have read in your life, all the worlds they've taken you to, all the characters you've met. Yeah, pure magic. Yeah, twenty-six letters.

I smile, I laugh, I tell jokes, I dance when the rhythm gets me, and I refuse to grow up, most of the time. I mean, don't get me wrong, I'm an adult when it is required, and I follow my responsibilities as if they're law. It's a great balance.

There's a couple of questions in my notes. *More about me? Describe your own personality?*

Okay. Where shall I begin? This isn't actually as simple as it sounds.

Erm …

I know what to do. If it comes up, and is relevant to the topic in hand, I'll add some details and information. A compromise. Yeah, compromises are useful.

Do you want to know something really amusing? I have no idea why I am writing this book, posting this blog, or working out how to make it a vlog or podcast. The idea originally stemmed from a conversation with a friend of ours, a child counsellor, yet it sparked a few embers in my mind.

I need to make a few points very clear, now, right from the beginning.

This IS NOT a self-help manual.

This IS NOT a guide on how to be a parent.

This IS NOT a guide on how to be a *better* parent.

This IS NOT full of chapters with detailed instructions on how to survive your life in parenthood.

I want to say it isn't going to take you out of a bad situation and put you in a great one, however, I can't actually know if those words will turn out to be true. You might read it and gain an amazing insight, decide to try a different method of approach when faced with a problem, or say, "At least I'm not the only one."

The change of tactics could solve it, or overcome an obstacle in your life. It happens. Perhaps, although again I can't be certain, knowing you are not alone will be enough.

You may feel less lost.

You may realise it isn't only you and your world. There are others.

The grass isn't always greener, and, this part is true, we all hide it from each other. We do. The school playground, the chat in town, or the posts on social media. We smile, we tell everyone we're okay, life is good, life is great. Not always the truth, though, is it? More often than not, it's easier to put on the mask than show the real face.

At the beginning I told you how I smile, laugh, tell jokes, and dance when the rhythm gets me. Guess what? I also don't smile, can't find anything to laugh about, am not in the mood for jokes, and want peace and quiet, not music.

Actually, there is more than a small part of therapy in the following journal. It's personal therapy, you know? I needed to get this stuff off my chest, so here it is. I'm also an author, and I love to help people whenever and however I can, so the three moulded together without a second thought.

Once you begin to write and document life, as and when it happens in a journal or diary, you can all too easily fall with Alice down the rabbit hole. You can open too many doors and have a choice of hundreds, even thousands, of paths.

Nature versus nurture.

Environmental and sociological factors on the upbringing of children.

Financial restraints, or decisions, and their impact on family life.

Don't worry, I didn't fall with Alice. All I have to say is modern parenting can be amazing, difficult, challenging, beautiful, stressful, frustrating, loving, upsetting, or, as it should be, wonderful beyond your wildest dreams.

Bear in mind, I started typing this introduction on the 10th of January, 2020, from handwritten notes I took at the end of 2019. For all I know, by the time I have finished, there will undoubtedly be some evolution, plus some new, or altered, reasons discovered. I'll undoubtedly change as the days pass by, I may have my own realisations. I also know how I write, the style I use, so I will edit this introduction many times, and I will add to it if and when it's required.

I need to return to 2019. In order to do that, I have to go back to 2018.

Every parent faces tough challenges. If you don't, please write your own book and wait for reviews calling you out as a fake, or enjoy the billions of pounds, dollars, or euros you will receive in royalties when it becomes an instant bestseller.

Normal day challenges can be logistical nightmares that involve you needing to be in four different places at once, at exactly the same time, while two children are ill, the electrician is coming to fix a plug socket, and you also have to get some money in the bank to pay an urgent bill. Or similar. Have you ever found out about a themed school day at half-eight in the evening?

"How long has this school letter been in your bag for?"

"I dunno. A couple of weeks?"

You then spend two hours trying to hunt down, create, or borrow clothes to fit said theme, all before your child cries for hours with disappointment and embarrassment.

The toughest challenges are usually related to 'real world' issues. Explaining the reasons behind hate, fear, or violence, can scare a child.

"It isn't a Disney movie out there. It probably never will be."

I've said those words a lot during the last decade.

Back to 2019. How was it for you all? Good? Bad? Amazing? Terrible?

Instinct wants me to shout the word terrible from the tallest building near me, but my spontaneity is always blocked by a ninja. A master ninja, trained in tactfulness, patience, and calm. She jumped inside my mind to check, and forced me to look at the past as a whole, not a single event.

Okay, the year had terrible parts to it, yet it also still had family, friends, laughs, and love. Plus dancing. Always shake those hips. Don't question it.

When you weigh it all up, when you list the pros against the cons, what are you really left with? I suppose this is an important point which I will return to many times in the book. This is also how I look at the world, every single day. *Every single day.*

If the good is always somewhere in your life, how powerful can the bad ever actually become?

Yes, I know, that sounds like such a cliché, an extremely annoying one, however, if you can find positives, they will always help you. Here's another annoying cliché. The good and positive, no matter how small or seemingly insignificant, provide you with a protective shield. They are your barrier, built to keep all the bad and upsetting away. The photo of you and your partner which brings back a special memory, the first cup of tea or coffee in the morning, the first cigarette, the chat with your best friend in the playground, a song, shooting the enemy on a computer game, a film, a show on television, your kid laughing or calling your name when you get home.

"Daddy back!" my youngest says when I see him, even if I haven't got back from anywhere. Then, a cuddle follows. "Aww, Daddy. You back."

How can I not smile? How? It is impossible not to. I'm not saying every bad thought will disappear, or the problems will be solved. I'm saying they will be less powerful. For that moment, that five minutes, however long the amount of time, you are protected. Wonderful beyond your wildest dreams, right?

The list could go on, couldn't it? I could fill a book with nothing but positives, *and, so could you*. The problem is, we could also fill one with negatives. Which book would have the most pages?

I was supposed to be telling you all about 2018, so I could get to 2019. You may have noticed I go off on a tangent sometimes. Imagine the winking face emoji, then the laughing emoji.

"It isn't a Disney movie out there."

I've already said it, yet it is relevant. There have been challenges for us before, as a family, as a couple, as individuals. This was definitely one of those.

Child, 13, ... Sawyer for the purposes of this project, then beginning his journey through senior school, ran into trouble. A push here, a shove there, the threat of a very real fight.

"Fuck off!"

"You fuck off!"

"Nah, mate, you fuck off!"

I couldn't decide how much detail to use here, so bare minimum it is, by default.

The following months, approximately four to five, were ... I can't use one single word, it won't be enough. School attendance was non-existent for Sawyer. A cruel introduction to fear and anxiety.

We panicked. We rang every professional we could

think of, or found on Google, or had recommended to us. Anger, frustration, hurtful words screamed in anger and frustration, fear, despondency, threats, punishments, regret. You name it, we experienced it.

Fortunately, it ended. It ended almost as abruptly as it began, however, we were all different because of it. The mental exhaustion, and mental wounds, took time to heal. Every subsequent disagreement, discussion, argument, they pulled us straight back, and it stills pulls at us now. We were scared of where they would take us, and are scared of where they *will* take us. Bridges burnt were slowly rebuilt, thankfully, and relationships mended. We were all different after, that much is true.

I'll take a brief moment to introduce the family, well, as much as I want to. I do believe it is time for some random names!

Obviously, I'm here. Insert winking face emoji, maybe a cheeky one with its tongue poking out for good measure.

Mum. We are madly in luurrve! She's so strong. Stronger than me, that's for sure.

Sawyer, you have already met. Then we have Leon, 11, Hugo, 9, and Jacob, 2.

Mum and I had decided earlier in the year to cut any unnecessary spending, *and* start to hit the bills. We were still paying for birthday and Christmas presents from the previous year, and it wasn't the first time. We would defer payments, pay off the old debts, then create new ones. Before you realise it, a vicious circle, and all too common these days. We're do-everything-we-can-even-if-it-means-we-miss-out parents, both from do-everything-we-can-even-if-it-means-we-miss-out families. That's common as well.

Due to this, Christmas 2018 was … I will use the words … financially careful. The children knew this. The children were warned about it. It still didn't make not getting a brand new games console any less painful. They're not spoilt, well, we don't think they are. How can they be when we have never had money to throw around? It's impossible to spoil if you don't have the money to back it up. As I said, we're do-everything-we-can-even-if-it-means-missing-out-parents. The issue here is that children don't fully understand, or see it working in the background. Misled, perhaps? They were given a good life from birth, even before, however, they didn't see the money moving about, the sacrifices made. Yeah, that sounds correct. Plus, they are bombarded with photos of amazing lives on social media. They want it. They want the same life. They want the clothes, the phones, the big house, and the custom-built computer.

"Dad?"

"Yeah, mate?"

"I just watched a video of a guy with the new iPhone X."

"… Okay."

"… So, can I upgrade?"

"… Erm … No. Sorry, mate. We can't afford that."

"Why not?"

"Well, we just can't. Bills, food. You know, all the boring grown up stuff."

"Yeah, but, that doesn't make sense. The guy I watched can afford it, and he lives in a big house as well. Why doesn't your job pay as much money as his?"

"I wish I knew," I would probably mumble.

"Pardon?"

"Nothing, mate. Nothing. So, what does this guy do, for work?"

"Posts videos."

"He posts videos?"

"Yeah. He posts videos. This one a few weeks ago was so funny! He ate a load of spicy food … a lot of people are doing it at the moment … I think it's called the Chilli Challenge, or something … Anyway, that's what he does. He posts funny videos."

"Okay."

At that point in the conversation, I'd either move myself to the kitchen and make a tea, apologise for not being able to afford a mobile phone, rant about underlying problems with the internet, social media, and appropriate role-models, or change the subject entirely.

So, the children had a quiet Christmas and New Year, and 2019 began. I won't walk the tangent line here again, yet I will give you an idea of 'normal'. Remember, this is my normal. Your normal will definitely be different. Almost everything about being a parent is subjective. It is never the same story. My list will differ from yours as much as yours differs from mine. Also, do not forget to weave in the wonderful beyond your wildest dreams. I don't want any reader to believe my life is a constant barrage of trials and worry. It is far from that, so very far from that. The wonderful is always there. *Always there.* Never forget the wonderful. NEVER!

First of all, they don't usually listen. Or, they listen after four hours when we start getting frustrated and angry at being ignored.

"Calm down, Dad. Why are you even annoyed?"

They argue with each other about trivial and unnecessary nonsense. Sometimes, it will escalate to an actual fight.

"Who scored the winning goal in the game we played on the X-Box six months ago?"

"Messi."

"No! Idiot! It was Neymar!"

"Messi!"

"Neymar!"

Yeah, seriously, that kind of trivial.

They hate the rules. We don't actually have many, if I'm honest. They still hate them. They complain about the school rules, sometimes, but respect them without hesitation. The threat of a timeout, a red card, a detention, or a visit to the headteachers office is enough. I often wonder why it is so different here, at home, but I'm yet to find the 'golden' answer.

They moan. We all moan, I know that, but they moan

a lot, and, *again,* it's trivial. It's also unfair and upsetting. For example, they don't like what is being cooked for dinner, yet won't suggest foods they do enjoy. We're blamed for this.

What else? They moan about the weather on the way to and from school, how hot or cold it is indoors, how tired they are, how bored they are, how hard their homework is, how slow the Wi-fi connection is when they're in the middle of a game or video, why the specific jumper they need isn't right at the front of the mess of clothes in the wardrobe, why they can't get through a certain level on a computer game. Yeah, I'm sure you get the point.

They rarely talk to us. No, that's misleading. They talk to us all the time. If it's important, though, we are usually the last to hear about it.

They know it all.

Okay, I'm sorry, you don't know it all. I don't and I'm in my mid-forties. Learning never ends. Every day is a day at school, that is another of my favourite sayings.
If they are proved wrong, they go back a couple of steps on the list and moan about it. It is usually our fault because we didn't teach them the correct information in the first place. To borrow a well used phrase ... Whatever.

Everything they want has to be done right now. Children think in minutes, maybe hours. They have little to no patience. Of course, this links together with the first point I made, and I have had thousands of discussions with the children about the unfairness of it all.

We are the default bad guys. They forget too easily about the wonderful beyond your wildest dreams, or anything similar. It's our fault.

I've had a great idea. Shall we take a quick break and play a game? Yeah, it will be fun, I promise.

How many 'roles' have you taken on from the following list? Being a parent isn't clear cut, trust me.

Teacher. Any and all subjects, even ones you have never heard of. Degree level understanding? No, Masters, to be on the safe side.

Nurse.

Doctor. Especially if the nurse above isn't sympathetic enough, or the splinter in their little finger is 'well bad!'.

Taxi. Bus escort. Train escort.

Bank manager. Of course, the unlimited pile of money. Every child knows about this is, so why won't they tell us all where it is?

Cook.

Cleaner. Housework duties.

Cleaner. Washing duties.

Cleaner. Everywhere else needing attention.

Personal shopper. While we're in town, we need to pick up a charging cable, football shin pads, swimming goggles, ketchup, but only the expensive kind and definitely not own-brand, school pens, chocolate, crisps which don't taste like feet, and the version of a console game released in 2017. Not 2018. Not 2016. 2017.

Referee. For those important decisions and arguments. I'll go right ahead and paste a line from above. *"Who scored the winning goal in the game we played on the X-Box six months ago?"*

Google.

Encyclopedia … of the ENTIRE universe.

Memory bank. You will be asked a question in regards to a Tuesday, in August, five to seven years ago, approximately. You must know the answer to this without hesitation or any form of study aid.

Carpenter, electrician, or general builder. This will depend on the situation.

Brake and gear specialist for all makes and models of bike.

Technological expert. If you can't wire up an iPhone to the Playstation, through the Xbox and television, but have the audio directed to Bluetooth headphones and the video streamed to a monitor in the bedroom, there's no point starting.

A pillow. No, an extremely comfortable pillow.

Weather forecaster. If it rains, or it's too hot, we should have warned them.

Alarm clock. A gentle and polite alarm clock. Children want to be woken up as if a cute kitten has crawled in the bed with them, purring with a gentle rhythm.

"Come on! It's seven o'clock! Up, breakfast, get dressed!"

How dare we? Such cruel and unusual parents.

Fun game, right? I've probably missed out more than I have listed. Oh, hairdresser! Yes, I mustn't forget hairdresser.

So, as far as memory serves, 2019 started off 'normal'. The balance was there, and everyone carried on with their days as per usual.

On the 25th of February, I received a telephone call. My mum rings every day, so it wasn't unexpected. I listened as she told me that my aunt, her sister, let's call her V, had been taken to intensive care. We immediately agreed to go to the hospital and see her.

V had a history of Chronic Obstructive Pulmonary Disease, (COPD). However, she still enjoyed too many cigarettes during the day. She still did too much around the house. She still worked at the age of seventy-two. A chest infection had literally floored her. She lost consciousness, was rushed to A&E, then transferred through to the intensive care ward.

I could write a lot here. I could, but I won't. I made the decision to be there as much as possible, and took work with me to the hospital on an almost daily basis. I spent a lot of time with V after she regained consciousness and was moved to other wards, and we smiled, laughed, and joked. She died, peacefully, on the 16th of March.

I am a positive person. I've already mentioned that part of my personality. Death really tests the theory. It *is* a test.

I passed, but only by the thinnest of threads. Anger consumed me. Sadness, frustration, bitterness, and my usual patience disappeared. The whole situation, still incomplete now, on the 10th of January 2020, almost broke me. I changed. Some of my 'light' faded. I don't know when, or if, it will ever burn as bright again. If I'm honest, I believe it will. I have to believe.

The subsequent months produced more of the same. V's will caused incredible tension and more anger. I could name people, call them out, all of it, but I won't. I have Facebook posts ready to go, and I will press the button one day. I will.

The reasons behind all the emotions? Betrayal, lies, secrets, and everything linking those together.

I feel a rant coming on. It's important. It's important because it is the reason, almost the main reason, why I put so much belief in 2020. I *needed* the new year, the new decade, to be different. It needed to be positive, there had to be a change, and I wanted to get rid of 2019 once and for all.

When I heard years ago, after my uncle David's death, that V had reconnected with an old 'friend', I was pleased. She hadn't smiled, not properly, in a long time. An affair began. It did. Deny it all you fucking well want to, *you know* I'm telling the truth. My mum knew, V knew what it was, all my side of the family knew. We even asked if we were about to get a new uncle and meet our new cousins. Yeah, it was seen as that serious.

After a while, when I asked any questions, I was told to leave it alone. It wasn't my business to pry. Sudden change of answer, in tone and in words, don't you agree?

I did as I was told. That's another one of the reasons for such strong feelings. He got to have his cake *and* eat it. He got to be married with a family and sneak around behind their backs, then inherit a house at the end of it all. I was so close to contesting the will. So close. Instead, I had to let him win. I couldn't risk the financial future of my family on a small chance of success. I had to let the lies, secrets, and betrayal win. I'm not surprised it almost broke me, and understanding why was important as well.

During this time, as I mentioned earlier, we had to face one of those 'real world', parent challenges. Death in the family, especially if it's the first experience for the children, can be horrific to understand. Dad changing didn't help. Dad changing from his usual calm and humorous self to an angered, bitter, sullen, and impatient man confused them, scared them, angered them as well.

Time heals. I believe it. Over time, I healed. I returned to my former self, almost fully, even though the entirety of my sadness, and every other emotion, still lingered inside. I was smiling, laughing, telling 'great' jokes again, and dancing to the music.

My birthday was in November. Forty-four years old. Wow! I mean, seriously, wow. I think I've 'lived', even though I haven't actually done a lot. Time also runs at a decent pace for me, if that makes sense? It isn't too slow, it isn't too fast. I don't feel as if it has sped up since I reached a certain age. Sometimes, though, the days, weeks, and months can blur together very easily.

My fiancée received a telephone call from her mum on the morning of my birthday. I know, you're probably feeling a sense of déjà vu, and, sadly, you are correct. Another family member was rushed to hospital. Another death to test us all. Poor kids. They didn't know either of the relatives well, yet they still had to deal with a terrible and upsetting year. The year who must not be named.

Could we get a fucking break? Seriously? Not a great day here, or a great day there, I mean weeks, months, of wonderful. It seemed the answer was obviously no.

Oh well, keep going, move on, deal with everything, heal, come out the other side.

We all hit auto-pilot in our lives, and it interests me when it takes over. I worked after V's passing, I went to town with the family, I did my share of the housework, however, I couldn't tell you anything specific.

I kept going, I moved on, I dealt with everything as best as I could. It's a strange blur with details scattered through. I expect it will all return to my memory one day.

I probably, almost-definitely-but-can't-be-sure, had the idea of this format for the project during the month of December.

A whole year. A whole account of one year in the life of a family. The wonderful beyond your wildest dreams, and the worst, most frustrating, upsetting times.

Thank you, reader, in advance, if you join me.

Chapter one

January

New Year's Day.

I've said it before and I'll say it again. Happy New Year!

I have already placed too much faith in this year, this decade, *and* I know it. I shouldn't set myself up in such a manner. I have a ... failure issue. I'll bring my positive emotions crashing to the ground when faced with nothing less than a difference from last year, and my shield will be put to the test. The fact I am aware should aid me if I choose to ignore it. *Should.*

Apart from some heated words caused by backseat gaming, though, I have nothing to write here. The children were all too eager to offer their 'advice' when one of them was playing on the console or computer. It doesn't go down well. Ever.

Still, wonderful beyond your wildest dreams threaded through the day. I love the holidays. I didn't use to, I dreaded them at one time in my life. Now, I love them. We are all together, and I can't get enough of it.

This is how I saw myself and the family during a previous daydream, one of the millions parents undoubtedly have, and it was made even more special because it came true.

2nd January.

Another one? Really? Two wonderful days in a row? Awesome!

I have a delayed stomach ache, and it's all my fault. I drank too much lager on New Year's Eve. Four cans isn't actually a lot, to be honest, but it was a special occasion.

Hugo has hibernated with his new games console, paid for with his own Christmas money, since the 26th of December. Throughout the day, he walked around the flat, grabbed snacks, told us about an amazing goal he scored, then disappeared again.

Jacob was his usual self. Believe it or not, he has a superpower. No matter the personal mood, the house mood, whatever, he will take it away with one smile, one laugh, or one of his cute sentences.

Leon mentioned he was excited to return to school. It's a relief to hear this because he has had transition issues from year six to year seven. Also, going back a few years, we didn't realise the extent of his anxiety. All children have a shy phase, all of them. Unfortunately, Leon's is more severe. It evolved, and, if you want a label, it is a generalised anxiety disorder. He had problems last year, yet we dealt with them. It was heartbreaking to see him panic, to lose himself to the fear, as he entered school. We persevered, we supported, he began to love his time there, and that is why his show of excitement meant so much.

Of course, he can still be a typical pre-teen as well. The plans for dinner were not to his liking today. He most definitely has a particular set of foods, and the word 'fussy' does not even begin to cover it. For too long, about an hour, he hovered near us, complained about how he was going to starve, how he *needed* to go over the road and buy a burger or a sandwich meal deal. In the end, he accepted his plan had failed.

Sawyer detests anything doctor, hospital, or health check related. He *never* asks for an appointment. Today, strangely, he did.

He described a mystery pain in his thighs, and it was only getting worse. We found out about a fall from his bike a few days before at one of the local parks. Nothing serious, the fall I mean, yet we wondered if it was the original cause.

After the doctor's assessment, hospital was recommended for further investigation. Mum packed a bag of essentials in a couple of minutes and off they went, despite some reluctance from Sawyer. We ignored it, and he was in too much pain to argue back.

By the end of the day, and I won't print any personal or medical details, a decision was made for emergency surgery, exploratory in nature.

Everything went well. Answers from surgeons and doctors. All good. Sighs of relief from everyone.

Jacob slept, despite missing Mum, yet Leon and Hugo were far too worried, inquisitive, or nervous to rest, so I went to bed and left them to chat.

I updated them to the best of my ability, whenever I could, but time was creeping on towards midnight.

We agreed years ago, when we began the family, that honesty is … usually … the best policy. I mean, occasionally, you have to make a judgement call, of course, but if I was told some news, they were as well.

3rd January.
Mum and Sawyer stayed at the hospital overnight, so I was at home with the other three children. We were all tired, and wanted news and updates beeping on our phones every few minutes. We knew it wouldn't happen like that, and I can tell you that it didn't, but we couldn't stop how we felt.

Okay, I just said we were all tired, didn't I? Despite all the above, Jacob was his usual superhero, energetic normal, and aware of the change in his own way.

"Where Mummy?"

"She's at the shops with Sawyer."

"Mummy yops?"

"Yeah. Shops."

Yeah, it tugs a little on the heart strings to hear those words. This holiday is going well, so well, unexpectedly well. Our family dynamic has been split, though, and there is a noticeable gap. We spend a lot of time here, and it is usually all six of us. Any change to the normal routine makes a difference.

While Leon was playing the console in the front room, he got excited about a race, or similar, and Jacob kept copying him, word for word. He has an old controller, without batteries, so he can 'join in'.

"Left!"

"Leh!"

"There! There! Faster!"

"Dere! Dere! Arter!

I had to smile and laugh when I heard it. Too cool. I decided to take him up the road for some fresh air and a treat. He does love a sausage roll.

Mum and Sawyer arrived home mid-afternoon. He was in a great mood, regardless of the pain, *and* his first experience of surgery.

Usually, he is easily angered, I mean, it's almost the default setting, you know? I guarantee I will return to his personality later in this journal.

Today, there was no impatience or frustration present. He was quiet, pensive, open to humour. In my notes, I scribbled the word epiphany. It wasn't an epiphany. He hasn't changed into a different person overnight because he had to deal with a serious event. Sawyer was simply taking some time to process the unexpected and suddenness of what happened to him. Don't forget the drugs floating around his bloodstream as well. The hospital administered strong medication during surgery, and after as well.

Other issues immediately arose, such as getting around the flat for everyday tasks, sleeping in a comfortable position, and travelling to and from school. We don't have all the answers, but we're trying our best to find them.

By the evening, tiredness gripped us all, so we enjoyed a quiet and relaxed few hours. We know Sawyer's recovery time is ahead of us, however long it will last.

4th January.

Slightly refreshed, however, I could still use a few more hours of sleep. Yeah, that was our morning motto today.

On the weekends, unless there is a good reason not to, Nanny and Aunt May visit us and the children. Yes, that is another random name. My mum and one of my two sisters.

They were kept in the loop in regards to news and updates about Sawyer, so understood his state of mind today. They were worried, yet relieved it wasn't too serious, and all over quickly.

Hugo needed to join me for a trip to town today, for new school shoes, but there was no desire to leave the games console cave of his own creation. But ... yeah, there's always a but. *He* wanted new shoes at the end of last term. *He* told us it would cause trouble at school. *He* asked us to take him to town straight after school. All of those worries have totally vanished now.

"I'm fine. I don't need them."

"I'll wear the black trainers."

"I won't get into any trouble with the teachers. Why would you think that?"

Nanny is all for treats, generosity, and helping out where she can. I get it from her and I try to teach the children exactly the same.

She decided to pay for lunch for us all. Burgers, fries, milkshakes and so forth. I was dubious as soon as it was mentioned, because the delivery company is **NOT** our favourite. Allow me to take a moment and tell you all a brief story.

A few months ago, because an entire order with enough food for six people was delivered as only two packs of fries, we had no choice but to refute payment.

For me, the jury is still out on all these new delivery companies. If something goes wrong, you try to contact the delivery company, but it borders on impossible. If you do, they blame the fast food outlet. If you contact the fast food outlet, they blame the delivery company. A strange void, an expensive and hungry one, is created for the customer.

Guess what happened next?

Yeah. Well done. The order was wrong. Again. Whichever Hogwarts House you belong to, take five points.

I think there may have been three packets of fries this time. Wow. The level of improvement was truly mind-blowing.

Not only did we get charged for this mess, the refuted payment I mentioned before was still floating around on their system, unpaid because of the refund. They recharged it to our bank. No lunch, but we paid for two orders.

Again, wow!

Disaster. Complete and utter.

Did I go out today? I actually don't know the answer to that question. I mentioned in the introduction about days, weeks, and months blurring together, so I guess this was one of those times.

5th January.

I know it sounds a bit sentimental, but we all had a lovely morning. Great conversation, and everyone was content. Even Sawyer, uncomfortable and in pain from recovery, filled his time with gaming or television.

The older children are due back at their respective schools tomorrow, except Sawyer. He will need a few more days, perhaps a week. They all attend separate ones, but we think it's a great idea. It gives them the chance to walk their own path. I'm unsure if Hugo will follow his two older brothers when he leaves primary, and pick a different senior school, but we will cross that bridge when we have to.

There is a birthday party later this afternoon, for one of Leon's close friends. She is turning twelve, and we are all invited because we're friends with her dad.

I decided to take Jacob to town for a few errands before I attend the party. It's a gaming party, so it's basically a room full of consoles. He enjoys staring at the televisions, pretending and trying to play, however, he also enjoys darting about between the seats and chairs. It is cute, funny, and adorable for all of ten minutes, then it grows boring, repetitive, and tiring.

Sometimes, you get a win. Sometimes, you are an amazing parent. I managed this in town with a couple of pairs of headphones! Haha! I returned a broken pair, replaced them with a better set, and bought another. Leon and Hugo were pleased with my choices. Win.

I stayed at home until near the end of the birthday party, and it all worked out. Jacob got to grab a slice of cake and some pizza, and we didn't have to chase him through the console maze.

Leon and Hugo had a relaxed evening as they packed their bags, found books, shoes, keys, calculators, plus loads of other junk which is only important to them and their school day.

I'm writing this from my notes, on the 22nd of January. If I look back in hindsight, with all honesty, I saw no signs.

None at all.

None.

6th January.

I briefly touched on Leon's anxiety disorder earlier, yet there is more to explain. So much more.

Leon has always been the shy kid. Well, no, not always, but the signs were there. The dynamic with our children always put him as the 'bad guy' in games, the one they complained about if it went wrong, the one against the two. I said this wasn't a self-help book, and it isn't, but we know it placed him in a certain mindset from an early age. Plus, he's empathetic, helpful, kind, and caring. Some would link those traits to being an 'easy target', and I could agree as well as disagree.

Yes, we put a stop to any bad behaviour when it happened, we educated so it wouldn't happen again, we punished when necessary. Despite those measures, although I will never be sure, had some of the damage already been done? Had some of the fear and triggering thoughts already started?

Once we realised, quite early on in year seven, that Leon was having problems adjusting to the transition, we immediately telephoned all the same numbers we had called when Sawyer had his issues. We arranged visits to the doctor, made referrals for youth mental health counselling, emailed the school, printed information off of websites, and found books we had purchased over the years, or bought new ones.

Sounds a bit drastic and extreme, I know. We could see it, though. We could imagine where the path headed and we didn't want to walk it, not again.

All in all, Leon only missed a few lessons from school. There was a 'mystery' ailment before the holidays, but it ran its course, thankfully. It was a virus focused in certain joints, however, it only added a few more days to the absence record. It was terrible timing, you know? One thing after another. A new worry. No break, once again.

We needed to take Hugo to school, so Leon joined us, nerves and all. We had a plan. In all honesty, he knew what we were going to do, but maybe all children believe their parents won't cross a line?

Drop Hugo off.

Head towards Leon's school.

Send text messages to understanding teachers, so help and assistance is ready when we arrive.

Keep calm. Keep conversation to a minimum.

We got him in. Once inside, enjoying lessons, Leon is

fine. Well, he copes. He finds his own ways to deal. It is the initial step creating such a strong barrier.

"I can't do it, Dad. I can't ... can't go through the gates. There's ... something stopping me."

It has been described as an invisible wall, a force much stronger than him, or similar.

We wouldn't be able to put the words here for how all this makes us feel, the toll it places on us mentally and physically. It is literally impossible. Too many emotions all punching, kicking, and shouting with incredible strength. Horrific is a good starting point.

I turn to my shield at every chance. I search for all the positives I can, and remind Mum of them as well.

Leon made it to school.

Leon will enjoy himself as soon as the panic passes.

Leon won't blame us for what we did.

Leon won't be like this forever.

Leon will be smiling tonight when I pick him up.

No, they don't always work. To use another annoying phrase, there is a 'light at the end of the tunnel'. I mean, one day, whenever that is, Leon will be able to control all of it. We *have* to see it, imagine it, and know it's a real possibility.

Childhood, eh? You are supposed to be full of sunshine, laughter, chocolate covered everything, running, falling over, getting up and running again, climbing trees, parties with too much food, love, sports day, friends, birthday and Christmas presents, riding bikes around the garden ...

Leon has all the above, and more. He smiles until his cheeks hurt, he laughs until his stomach hurts. He also sees a darker side. The one with too many questions, too many negatives, so much *might* happen. There is caution, there are also fears impossible to avoid or ignore.

This might be one of those times when I have to type out some personal information. I currently suffer from diagnosed anxiety. I had counselling, I tried all the techniques, and some worked. I now continue to practice calming methods, and also take medication. I do blame myself, more than I want to, for Leon's condition. Remember the 1st of January? I'll copy the line to remind you all.

I have a … failure issue.

I must make this very clear. I do not 'show' my anxiety in front of the children. Yes, I teach them common sense, and caution, but they have never seen me in the grip of a panic attack.

I never discovered an underlying event, or situation, or trauma, that caused it. It just … happened. I'd easily say it took my entire thirties away from me. Everything was coated in it. Every party, every plan made, every thought outside my normal routine.

So, how do I see the situation? My own knowledge and experiences can be used to help Leon. Positive. It's all my fault. I blame myself. Excuse me while I add another failure badge to my collection. Negative. Excuse me, again, while I flip a coin.

Leon's help is in the pipeline. When? No idea. That wasn't supposed to sound sarcastic, I actually don't know the answer. There has been an initial assessment so far. I admit, I wanted medication prescribed for him there and then. Instinct takes over.

Protective parent incoming!

Take cover!

All the help, right now. Not tomorrow, not the following week.

Right fucking now!

Mum and I often ask where our help is in all this. We did before when Sawyer was experiencing his issues. Unfortunately, it is worrying to consider. Yes, there are meetings, groups, counselling, and friends. There is also crippling embarrassment, our own anxieties, stress, feelings of failure, and wearing one of those masks we spoke of earlier.

"Yeah, we're all good. How's you?"

At its most basic level, all any parent wants to know,

to believe, is they're doing something. They aren't useless. They are helping, and they can help, even when it seems they can't.

Plus, don't forget, our panic, our agitation and anger, it ripples through the house. Others notice the change in mood, and it threads through all of our lives. It's quite common, even if you don't realise it. I'll try and explain.

Imagine a day in your life, okay? We're going to make it an annoying one, though. Sorry about that.

So, where shall we begin? You're getting ready for the school run, brushing your teeth in the bathroom. You accidentally drop the lid, bend down to pick it up, then bump your head on the sink. You might laugh it off, but for the sake of this example, you don't. You get pissed off. Great start to the morning.

Ten minutes up the road, you realise you have forgotten your purse or wallet. You really needed to go to town and stock up on food, ready for the week.

"Damn it! Now I've got to go back home after the school run."

"Mum! I forgot my lunchbox."

"What?"

"I forgot my lunchbox."

Now you have to go back home, grab your purse or wallet, *and* the lunchbox. You have to go back to school to drop it off, then go to town.

The changed morning is dealt with, and you get home with a couple of bags of shopping.

Wait a minute. There's a card through the post. You've missed a delivery!

"Damn it!"

Guess where the delivery office is? Yeah, back in town. Guess what? It just started to rain. Guess what? You have a headache coming on.

You pick the child, or children, up later that afternoon, and head home. You've had enough now. All you want to do is get dinner out of the way, soak in a hot bath, watch television for an hour or two, then sleep.

"I can't wait to get home and try on my new goggles! I can show everyone tomorrow when we go swimming."

"Swimming goggles? Oh, damn it!"

"What? You forgot? You knew I had swimming this week!"

"I'll sort it, okay? Don't get upset with me! I've had a terrible day today. I've walked for bloody miles. There's a pair in the cupboard at home, I just need to move all the heavy boxes about to find them."

"What's for dinner?"

"Pizza."

"Again? We had pizza at the birthday party on Saturday. Can I have pasta? Or nuggets and curly fries?"

"No, it's pizza! Okay? Stop moaning about dinner! You've been out of school for two minutes and you've already blamed me for forgetting your goggles, and now you're going on about food!"

Here, we stop. Here is where the whole point of this example becomes clear.

The day made you annoyed. The day pissed you off. The day was full of events that could have gone better.

How much of that annoyance and anger came out because of that simple question about dinner? Dinner might have pushed you over the edge, but it was one part of a larger picture. The child, or children, in school for the day had no idea about any of it.

I'm guilty of this here. We're all guilty of it here, my children included. What I'm trying to say is … erm … how to put it into words? If the reason, or reasons, for the anger are not in front of you, be it a person or an object (like the toothpaste lid and sink. Haha!), then why are you shouting at someone, or something else?

Shall we go back to the point where we are on the school pick up? We can try a different ending this time.

"I can't wait to get home and try on my new goggles! I can show everyone tomorrow when we go swimming."

"Swimming goggles? Oh, I completely forgot those, and I've been to town twice. I'm sorry. We do have some at home. You can help me lift a few boxes around later."

"Are you sure we have some at home?"

"Yes, I promise."

"Okay. So, Why did you go town twice?"

"Shopping, and I missed a delivery. I had to go back down in the rain. It's been one of those days."

"Yeah, we had indoor play."

"Oh, that's cheeky! You get to stay dry and warm, and I get soaked."

"Haha! You got wet! You got wet!"

"Cheeky!"

"What's for dinner?"

"Pizza."

"I had pizza on Saturday, at the birthday party. Can I have pasta? Or nuggets and curly fries?"

"Hmm? I'll make a deal with you, okay? You help me look for the swimming goggles, then I'll cook pasta tonight. Sound good?"

"Yay! Pasta!"

I know, I know, these are two random examples I just made up. However, I know which I'd prefer.

Here's an interesting note. I can't remember when I searched for a home schooling website last year. It would have been at some point in September, I believe, but it was still open on my phone's browser. Even if I could use it as a temporary measure, until it's a managed state and under control.

So, the thought turns to failure again.

Why failure?

I am no bestseller. I work fucking hard, trust me. Twelve hour days aren't uncommon, sometimes longer. I also wear many different hats in my job. Marketing, sales, social networking, new markets, writing, editing, design, formatting, filing, order placement.

Hey, I'm not complaining. No, I love it! Love it! Did I make the correct choice, though? Should I have found a different line of work, instead of putting everything into self-employment?

I don't have the money to try out my theories to help Leon. I should have, because of my responsibilities as a parent. Don't misunderstand me, money doesn't solve problems, and I'll never believe that to be true. I can't help but wonder what I could, and would, do for others if I had the means.

After all the fear this morning, there was a smile on Leon's face as he came out of school. I cannot tell you how much it changed my mood. I sent a text to Mum, so she could smile about it as well.

His new headphones went on, music played, then Leon disappeared into a playlist. There were smiles and jokes on the way home.

This is another fascinating trait which interests me. How do we all find our safe place? Why do most of us need one?

As you have already seen from a lot of the previous pages, the difference in regards to attitude and demeanour can be striking at times. It's also misleading. It's most definitely inspirational.

Leon fights hard with the mundane, the normal, the situations a lot of people wouldn't give a second thought. I wish he saw that strength. We definitely see it.

I tried to research post-surgery hygiene routines for Sawyer. It was a bombardment of interesting, comical, ludicrous, and practical. The internet can be such a strange place at times.

Laughing emoji. Winking face emoji. Roll my eyes emoji. Wow, I use the latter so often, I'm surprised my eyes don't hurt more. Anyway, I decided to work late today. Hugo is moaning at me right now, as I make notes. He wants my help to search for something, yet the impatience has kicked in.

Shit! Shit! Shit! Fuck it!

All was fine. The wonderful was here. We all felt it. I was being sarcastic about their football team, laughing, and winding them up a bit. It's too easy at times, but taken in the right way.

Then, it all went wrong. So wrong.

Leon sat down with Jacob.

Leon and Jacob bounced too close to Sawyer.

Sawyer panicked. He was worried about Jacob unintentionally jumping on him after the surgery.

Sawyer screamed at Leon, then pushed him off the sofa.

I stepped in to diffuse the situation and asked what was going on. Referee time.

The argument started.

It was bad. It was terrible. It was emotional. Tears. Words screamed in anger. Imagine the absolute worst words you can. They were all said, shouted, or yelled, mostly at me.

Sad doesn't come close.

We stayed calm and tried to diffuse the moment. Yes, we raised our voices, but you have to sometimes, just to be heard over the others involved.

It all seemed to be focused on me. I said something to cause the escalation in anger. The problem is, though, I have no idea what it was. I don't think I'm ever going to find out.

Unfortunately, Sawyer disappeared to his room. He doesn't want to talk to me now, and we didn't see each other for the rest of the evening.

I tried to wind down by watching television with Mum and Jacob, but my mind was on the argument. I didn't sleep until late because of it.

7th January.

This is how I imagined today. I would work, base level and extras as well. Loads of it. Keep it coming. Pile it on my desk until I can't see the monitor. Writing, editing, new chapters, new books, blog posts, record and post videos about new chapters and new books.

How about … erm … no?

I know this is starting to sound like a repetitive series of events, however, if you understand, then you understand. Understand?

Once any family becomes trapped in the vicious anxiety circle, it is difficult to escape.

Leon knew he was going to be nervous, and he told me as much. He warned me, bluntly, about the fear he was experiencing. He could sense it getting stronger as every minute ticked by.

We left the house at the usual time, arrived at school with about ten minutes to spare, then it hit hard. It was crippling and paralysing, right outside the gates.

When I walked one step towards Leon, he would walk two back.

"Dad, you're scaring me! Stop! Stay there! Don't get any closer."

I need to pause here for a second. This is an important point to make. It is about actions, responding to those actions, and seeing what is *really* there. Ignore what you see or hear, it's a twisted version of the truth.

Let me try and explain. Leon knew I was trying to help him, encourage him, support him, and overcome the panic by his side. Instead, he treated me like an enemy. He told me I scared him, then ordered me to stay away. How I respond to his actions is the important point. I could tell him to stop being silly, I could become offended, I could grow angry, I could grow upset, I could show him how his actions are to blame for my responses. I could even twist the blame around and add even more stress to his already burdened young mind. All I'm saying is be careful. Please, be *very* careful. Think about every word or action before you say it or carry it out. See what is really there, yeah?

I've failed at this. It's easier to fail than succeed, I

believe, because it is so difficult. I failed this morning, so it's relevant. I couldn't tell you how, I can't remember, but I know it happened.

My only advice is stay calm and, again, see what is really there.

Several teachers came out to the gates to offer their support. It has helped in the past, and it also proves one of my beliefs. Teachers are rockstars, and they provide so much in modern education.

I notify Mum, so she will meet me in a while, and Jacob will be there as well. We do worry about how he perceives all of his older brothers. What will he learn from them? How does he process everything he sees?

At nearly eleven there were quite a few of us by the gates, including attendance staff offering even more support and understanding. We agree to call it for the day, and arrange for future telephone calls, emails, or meetings.

The walk to or from school usually takes approximately thirty-five minutes. I don't remember if it ended up lasting more than that, but it was a tough one. Leon and I had been standing in the cold for close to three hours, so our legs were numb and as heavy as concrete. He studied and completed homework for the rest of the day, and retreated inside himself somewhat. Quiet, overthinking the events of the morning, and self-reflective.

Sawyer and I thought of brilliant and inventive methods to bath or shower post-surgery. The entire situation morphed into a comedy masterclass. It involved cutting plastic shopping bags, putting chairs in baths, putting towels in baths to support said chairs, and about an hour of planning before a drop of water even came out of a tap.

In case you were wondering, he spoke to me normally, as if the previous evening's argument never even happened.

Hugo and Leon fought with each other before bed. Punches were thrown as well, however, it was sorted out quickly.

Leon was guilty and apologetic about the incident, and rightly so. He knew there was blame to carry. Hugo will always lose it if his brothers call him certain names. They are not overly offensive or cruel, more teasing if anything, but he detests hearing them.

Years ago Hugo had a seizure. Thankfully, it was an isolated episode, and he's had loads of tests carried out since. All negative, you'll be glad to hear. The fight caused a painful headache, though. I didn't say anything about the seizure, Hugo didn't mention it either, but I had a feeling we were both thinking about it, and it worried him enough to delay sleep.

I ended the day boring him to sleep with a random story from my life, or similar. It usually works. I'm not boring, though, I promise!

8th January.

Leon got out of bed, walked to our bedroom, sat back down, then, with a look on his face I have seen so many times before, he stared at the school uniform. I told you there was repetition, didn't I? I told you there was a vicious circle.

I love déjà vu sometimes in life, it's another fascinating aspect. Today, it punched me in the stomach, then the face, then it … I don't know … called me ugly as well.

Normal clothes on, then Hugo's school run. If we make him wear uniform now, it's always a 'scam', exactly the same as Monday was.

During the walk, I searched for answers and pushed for them, encouraged Leon to open up, but the enthusiasm wasn't there. Still, you have to try, you have to look for those elusive answers.

Back at home, strict rules were stated. The past, specifically Sawyer's absence I mentioned in the introduction, taught us both to make them clear from the beginning. Acceptable, not acceptable. Easy, right?

No mobile phone during the day. Only at lunch or break, as per school.

No television.

No games console time.

No computers, unless school test related.

Leon must use his time in a constructive or educational manner. Reading books, homework, any tests available online from school, or subject websites.

Mum also signed up for online lessons on a trial basis.

Easy, right? I asked that two seconds ago, and now my eyes hurt because I just rolled them again.

Leon said no. Leon hated the idea. Leon couldn't find a decent book from the hundreds to choose from here, not to mention others on the Kindle.

"Nah. I've checked every bookshelf. Nothing interests me. They're all rubbish!"

I printed off a reading list provided by Leon's school. I own about half of them.

"Nah. I'm not reading any of those."

I had a premonition today. All parents can use 'The Force', we know that's true. We can see situations involving our children before they happen. Mine was that Leon will be off school for a while. He has found a dark place, and we aren't … I don't know what the word is here. Prepared? Able? Qualified? It's a mixture of all those, plus several hundred others.

Anxiety is a personal issue, a personal fear. Whatever Leon's mind is going through, it is a real fear to him.

Another dilemma presented itself for the rest of the morning. The behaviour grew unacceptable. Sawyer wasn't at school either, so he also decided, against our wishes, to add his own brand of advice.

Leon swore, punched the floor, or lashed out at wardrobe doors a few times, thus creating the dilemma. Yes, he is confused, frustrated, unable to control powerful emotions, but he is also nearly twelve and pubescent. See what is really there. See what is *really* there.

We saw unacceptable behaviour and resistance to our new rules. Wasting time. Causing trouble as a distraction.

There are so many answers here, so many different

ways to handle it. We chose to stay firm. No matter what else is going on, he cannot swear at us, he cannot become violent, and he cannot dictate his terms to us. We could have tried talking through to calmness, understanding, or allowing it *because* of the anxiety. We didn't, and I don't believe we will regret it.

"Right, let's go to town and buy some books. They have loads to choose from. It will stop you falling behind for when you get back to school," said Mum.

Leon wouldn't leave the house because we had his mobile phone. It was handed over as part of the new rules.

"I need it! What if I get lost? What if something happens and I need to ring someone?"

There were more questions and reasons not to leave, all repetitive in nature. Leon didn't realise he was caught in a loop.

All of the fears were unfounded, unnecessary, and irrelevant, except to him. They're real for him.

He cannot get lost because he knows the town and streets very well. The chances of some terrible event hurting three of his family are … mathematicians and statisticians can work on that for me.

So, irrational, yes. Believed, also yes. A subconscious attempt to undo the punishments and rules? I can't answer.

We cancelled the town visit and Leon went for a shower to calm down.

On the school run for Hugo, I talked to Leon about invisible enemies. It's a reference to a book we bought three years ago. An amazing teacher noticed the anxiety. He noticed it was more than shyness and normal nerves, then took Leon under his wing and pushed gently with his confidence. It worked.

I know Leon is open to advice. Some children ignore everything when parents start talking, deliberately or not. You can literally tell from his facial expressions that he has reached a new level of understanding.

"Listen, mate. You are not scared of a building. You

are not scared of children, and you are not scared of teachers. You are worried about the unknown part of it all. What might happen. You are … scared of being scared."

It is *so* much more difficult to fight an invisible enemy, especially if it can cause physical changes. Their heart thumping too fast, feeling as if they can't breath, legs too weak to move, to name a few.

You can't see it, or touch it, but you know it's there, waiting to strike and take control.

Can you see the evening routine? I noticed it as I typed and edited this, on the 29th. Once the set times for schoolwork pass, everyone feels more relieved and relaxed.

The evening was calm and we all found our happiness. Moments such as those, quiet, together, all the children enjoying themselves, are made of pure gold. I wish for more, I covet them.

9th January.

The uniform problem is now officially 'a thing'.

We went to town and bought the textbooks we wanted to pick up yesterday. Over thirty pounds in total for English, mathematics, and science, the core curriculum subjects.

If Leon is here, he will be learning, or doing his best to try. The online lessons we signed up for yesterday were only a trial, so we cancelled them in advance, in favour of the textbook format.

I went to see my mum and May today for a few hours. The childhood home always makes me smile. We didn't have a lot as a family back then, but I remember all the great times.

Mum telephoned me. The attendance staff visited Leon while I was out, to see what he was doing. To see the situation for themselves. They informed Mum that we need a signed note from either the doctor or therapist. They want him declared medically unfit for school attendance.

Erm … okay? I think?

We left a message with our youth mental health team and hoped it wouldn't be too long before a reply came back.

Again, one of the coveted evenings followed. Leon worked hard all day, without problems. I spoke to him about it, and told him to try and live 'in the moment', not too far ahead. I also explained about finding positives and using them to help, for example, all the studying he enjoyed while I was out.

10th January.

Do you remember 2018 from the introduction? Our decision to start paying off all the debts instead of adding to them? Well, one of the main reasons for all of the financial wizardry, an end goal, is so we can move out of the flat.

We need more room. We need it. Need it!

Currently, we have a flat with two bedrooms. Yeah, you've counted correctly, there are six of us. It can be great. All the family bundled together. Aww, how cute. Or, it can be horrible. I wish I had some fucking space in here!

I saw a couple of larger properties today, on our agent's website. One was out of price range, the other in price range, and only a couple of minutes away. Easy to carry boxes, right?

I decided to be a detective and went across the road to investigate. I've always been promised better behaviour if there was more space for us all to live in.

The children have grown up in the same room for their whole lives, apart from the cot days. I completely understand, I do. If I think about it for too long, I wrestle with the failure complex again. We wouldn't be in this situation if I had made different choices, or worked for an extra hour, or pushed harder when I had my sales hat on.

It turned out the property had already been let, so my detective work was a complete waste of time. Still, searching, searching again, giving up because you're bored of searching, it is all commonplace when looking to move home.

I opened my music app, turned up the speaker, and

the music played for hours. We sang, danced, then sang and danced some more. It was an amazing Friday evening.

I spoke to Leon at the end of the day, briefly. He was already worrying himself about Monday morning. I didn't want such thoughts covering his entire weekend and ruining it. I simply told him to try and put the uniform on for five to ten minutes, no more. It would still be a battle won.

My notes have a few lines about guilt and apologising. I've already told you about Leon's personality. If he thought his actions were upsetting me, or his mum, it would make him feel incredibly guilty. I don't remember details of the late conversation, but it must have happened. I expect it was a few, sincere words.

"Sorry about all the stress this week, Dad."

"Oh, that's okay, mate. We understand, I promise."

11th January.

Nanny and May over again. It's a very cool family relationship, so it guarantees fun and laughs for all. My mum is in her late-seventies, so has a very down-to-earth outlook on the world, and life in general.

Unfortunately, we tend to talk about V. It's inevitable and I expect it will be for some time. The conversations often head in such a direction because of coincidence, purpose, or the residual emotions. The bitterness we all feel simmers under the surface.

The will was discussed, so curiosity sent me to Google. V's address brings up an estate agent's website, and the property was listed. I took a few moments with Nanny and Mum to go through the photographs. Yeah, strong memories lingered.

If I'm reading the information correctly, it is no longer for sale, off the market. It's over. The bungalow has gone. Sold.

An immediate dark mood takes hold of me. I'm upset, of course, and a headache appears as well. I keep it hidden, and try to lighten the mood with Nanny. Jokes always help. Calling certain people 'Cheating, thieving, liar,' also helps a great deal.

I don't want to bring the house mood down with me, though, so I hide the emotions away inside. I'll mumble under my breath later and let it out.

Sawyer went out to meet friends in town, *and* he took his bike. He was advised in the hospital not to exert himself, not to undertake any strenuous activity. We reminded him, but it fell on deaf ears. I understand, I really do. He's missed his friends, being social, and moving around normally. He also knows the recovery process lasts longer than a couple of weeks, though, *plus*, riding a bike after surgery relating to the legs is a terrible idea!

Mum and Nanny went to the shops with Jacob. About five minutes later, Leon started to ask me if I was going to meet them.

"No, mate. Why?"

"I wanted to go with them."

"Okay. You can if you want to. They're only up the road. You know the shops, you'll find them no problem."

Leon shifts about in the hallway.

"I … don't want to go out on my own today."

A new symptom? It's new for me to hear, let's put it that way.

Leon doesn't have a problem with going out. He disappeared to the local park for three days in a row recently, all on his own. He enjoyed himself for a few hours each time, caught up with some friends, and flew about on his bike. It was great to see his red cheeks and excited smiles.

Can anxiety change so quickly? Why is it reaching through other parts of his life? Is his inability to fight allowing it to spread? I know, I know, strange questions.

Is there an 'I told you so' emoji? Sawyer called, so I want one. He was in pain, and had stopped approximately ten to fifteen minutes from home.

"I can't walk any further! I'm having trouble riding the bike because it's too windy."

I was fixing Mum's mobile phone at the time. No, I was *attempting* to fix Mum's phone, even though it seemed like a lost cause. She met with Sawyer and they inched their way home, almost literally.

He laughed about it, a little, then slumped on the sofa to rest.

Wonderful beyond your wildest dreams definitely won today. I know I fell towards a dark place while thinking … overthinking … V's house, but my shield did not break. This is why I use it. This is why I created it in the first place. This is why I look at the world with the eyes I do. I never know when I will need it, or how strong it will need to be.

12th January.

Last night, everyone except Sawyer was told to be up and ready at a decent time this morning. We had a trip to town planned and wanted to get moving.

We always hope it will be enjoyable for the children. They do have some money to spend, so that always helps. If we're only going to shops for food, or practical reasons, it can be boring for them. Bored children equals many different things.

Feel free to take a moment to think of your own. Ours often tell us how tired they are, how hungry they are, or they start moaning at each other. Or, they can enjoy themselves as we hoped they would.

"You're not tired. I didn't fall asleep until after eleven last night. You're not as tired as I am!"

Referee! Call the referee!

Suddenly, as we're about to walk out of the door, Leon started to look for a bag to take with him. Trust me, this was confusing.

Leon wanted to buy a new art set. He'd seen it on a previous visit to town. He really enjoys art. It also calms him, distracts him, and gives him something positive to focus on.

"Why do you need a bag?"

"To put the new art set in."

"Okay. They'll give you a bag at the shop, when you buy it. No worries. Let's go."

"No, you don't understand. I need a rucksack … to put it in after I buy it."

"Erm … take your school bag."

"Yeah. I suppose so."

Someone then mentioned it was too small. Back to square one. Leon grew more and more agitated.

"Mate, calm down. You want a bag to carry the art set in, but one with straps, so you can wear it on your back?"

"Yeah, that's what I need!"

"Erm … we don't have anything like that … at all. We've never had anything like that in the house. It can't be done. You'll just have to come, or stay here."

Yeah, I know. Ultimatums aren't helpful or useful. I grew impatient and frustrated too easily, but I could see how upset Mum was. She enjoys the visits to town so she can unwind, take Jacob out, and lose herself to window-shopping daydreams.

I said it was confusing, didn't I?

I can't remember when we decided it, but we always told the children that their behaviour, regardless of the reasons for it, wouldn't ruin any plans. They won't change anything, even if they believe their actions will.

I quickly spoke with Mum and agreed I'd go out anyway. I don't want to leave her, but we both understand the method.

As soon as I was out of the house with Jacob and Hugo, text messages started to arrive by the second. In my notes, I guessed twenty. I then opened up my messages and checked the actual number. Thirty. Thirty messages.

Almost all of them were erratically typed nonsense, with a couple here and there that asked me to come back. I told myself not to turn around. I did not turn around.

As we reached town, Mum sent me a photo message. The dining table had collapsed after being leant on.

Yes, I'm being serious.

46

"Hey, Universe."

"Hi, Blake. How's it going?"

" … "

"What?"

"You know what."

"Listen, I can't stop and chat. I'm, like, super-busy today. I spilt a cup of tea all over some files this morning, so I need to clear them up."

"Yeah, yeah, you go be super-busy."

"I'm sure your file was on my desk. Wow! I'm, like, really sorry about that."

" … "

"Chat soon, Blake."

Fortunately, the dining table only made a mess and there were no injuries. Well, a splinter, I think. I carried on with Jacob and Hugo.

Don't forget, we're still in the confusing stage. Part two is about to begin.

Leon calls me. Sawyer said he would bike into town with him, so, of course, EVERYTHING IS FINE NOW.

What? Why? How? WHAT!?

We need to understand this. We need to understand this better. Panic to calm in the blink of an eye. Oh, yeah, I thought it as well. What many of you just thought. It's exaggerated. It's faked. It's a tantrum to get his own way. If I hadn't witnessed it with my own eyes, I'd follow the idea. Plus, what would 'his own way' be in this case? I can't think of one. He wouldn't have gained anything by staying here.

I told Leon he wasn't allowed to leave until he helped Mum with the table.

Town worked, eventually, although Mum missed out on all of it. So unfair. We're in this together, and I don't mean today and this situation. I'm talking about our life together. There should never be a time when either of us feel alone.

Back at home, I make it clear to Leon he needs to work through an anxiety book we own. There are exercises, methods, and lots of interesting help authored by intelligent people. These intelligent people have already spent years training, so they know what they're talking about.

Immediate refusal.

I make notes in the book, change some of the more difficult terms, and highlight the parts I want Leon to read.

Immediate, angry refusal.

"I hate the book. It's disgusting! Get it away from me before I'm sick."

Now, I spoke a moment ago about exaggeration and similar traits. I know this is simply reluctance mixed with behaviour, however, I also know my children. Leon is scared of being scared, remember? The book represents difficult thoughts, guilty thoughts, apologetic thoughts, fearful thoughts, and he doesn't want them. We will keep trying.

I gave Leon some of his calming medicine. Once it settled him, I spoke about the consequences of too much stress on such a young mind. I also assured him it is always multiplayer. He is never on his own, or single-player. Mum, Dad, Leon. Multiplayer.

I didn't mention the shield by name, yet I did break down the fundamentals for him. Maybe if he works on his own shield, such as music, television, film, interests, activities, memories, he can fight back? Can he protect himself? Has he *already* got one, but it's failing him?

After dinner, I was tired, Mum was tired, and Leon was exhausted. He mentioned to me that his head is now evil. I borrowed a Harry Potter reference and compared it to a Boggart in the wardrobe.

"Riddikulus!"

That's right. Call it something stupid. Call it something ridiculous. Take its power away.

I asked for five to ten minutes in the school uniform tomorrow. I'm not interested in actually going to the school, or trying to get him into any lessons.

We wish we knew why he has travelled so far back. I mean, at the beginning of year seven, it wasn't this bad, so why has it become so strong now?

We will move on, forward, step by step. We have to change and adapt as soon as the symptoms do, even *before* they do.

It's multiplayer. Always multiplayer.

13th January.

Mum decided to push for the help we are waiting to receive, because yesterday was so difficult for Leon.

Our doctors surgery opens at eight in the morning. If you get there in person, you can book an early appointment, or, if necessary, be seen straight away. Mum booked one for 9:20am.

Leon came back to the flat, then Mum went out for another early errand. Sometimes, we are busy here, super-busy, like the Universe. Winky face.

I had a feeling Leon would be worried about the appointment. No, let's be honest here, I *knew*. He kept asking me for the Wi-fi password.

"I need to disappear with some fun and silly videos for a bit. It calms me down, Dad."

I believe him. Of course I do. It's an exact example of the positives in the shield. Glad to know he was paying attention, but I can't take all the credit. Looking back, he's been using the same technique for years now. He *already* has a shield.

Yesterday's misbehaviour with the anxiety book caused me to take Wi-fi away, though. I needed to stick to my rules at this point. It definitely wasn't coming back. He owed me something first. I didn't care what it was.

As I left the house with Jacob and Hugo for the school run, Leon panicked. He didn't want to be here without Wi-fi, and he definitely didn't want to be here on his own.

That reminds me. Sawyer returned to school today. Let's get a round of applause. Well done, mate!

Wait. He went on his bike? Shall we all sigh together?

"You'll be fine, mate. Fresh air and a walk will clear

your head, ready for work later," I said to Leon.

I got him out and shut the door. Let me say, I was not in the good books. I used a variety of tactics to achieve my plan. Tough persuasion, as in the dreaded ultimatums, encouragement, and quick hand movements to grab the door. Once he was outside, I started walking, so he had no real choice but to follow.

"How could you do that to me? I thought this was meant to be multiplayer? You said it was! You said it last night!"

I spoke to Hugo more on the way up the road. It is important to share our time equally between all the children, yet even we can become distracted. He is only nine. He may act more mature, but he is still *only nine*. I don't want to imagine how he perceives what is happening.

I met up with Mum at the top if the road, explained why Leon wasn't in a great mood, then they went off to the appointment. He will forgive me for my 'sneaky' actions earlier.

So, he can't be signed off, not by the doctor. Many phone calls followed, and some were contradictory, or at least some of the information was. This is so annoying, this part of the 'process'. As parents, and the children involved, you are placed in a void. School, the doctor, the mental health team, they all work behind the scenes while you float along, usually unaware of what is happening, or what will or might happen next. It's a worrying place to exist. You believe you're not doing everything possible, what you are doing is wrong, or you may even be punished for it as well.

A meeting was booked for tomorrow with our support, EWMHS (Early wellbeing and mental health services), to see if we can move forward somehow. Plus, if there is an opportunity to ask for advice, take it. There are always questions. Of course, you may have a different path to follow with a different service or organisation.

As we see it, school are content to let the situation run and assist the process along the way. As I said about the void, it's extremely important to remind yourself that all involved have a set protocol, and they usually stick to it. Their rules and regulations do not change because you want them to.

One of the telephone calls Mum took upset us both. I contacted a known member of staff to let them know I was becoming disappointed with certain aspects of it, and disagreed with them as well.

Don't be afraid to question decisions. Don't be afraid to disagree. They give advice, yet they sometimes word it in a certain manner. It can sound as if they are pointing the blame, or cause, towards us as parents. Our methods aren't working, we need to change them. Our own anxieties and frustrations are teaching habits to the children. Stop that right now if you can, you're making it worse.

It isn't a simple task, so I won't pretend it is. The lesson here, or point I'm making, is to question that which you need to, especially if there is any disagreement. You're with the children, or child, all the time. All the time. You are qualified when it relates to your children. You don't follow a set of questions, or a timeline, or a book. You're living with it. It's now. Right now. In this very moment. There's a flip side, because, you know, there's always a flip side. You're too involved, because you are there all the time.

Oh, I just fell into the void.

So, I can't be objective, because I spend too much time with the child.

When I do spend time with the child, I have to be careful about every word I say, or how I act.

Eventually, professional help will arrive. It could be their school, a doctor, or a counsellor. Or all three. Or two. Can't say when, though. In the meantime, change your entire personality for me.

The evening was quiet. Wonderfully quiet. Gloriously quiet. We found time to talk with each other, and not just about family matters. We both seek out moments such as those, or purposely find them, and it's an absolute miracle at times.

The only trouble I mentioned in the notes was about Leon's old mobile phone. He upgraded after Christmas to a newer model.

Remember my unsuccessful attempt to repair Mum's phone a few nights ago? It didn't work, so while she is sorting out a new one, she borrowed Leon's. She volunteers with an organisation involved with many parenting groups, support groups, and child events, so her messages fill up fast.

It bothered Leon, though. He wanted to help, but he also wanted a backup. Unusual, although I can almost see the reasoning behind it. The safety net. An integral part of his own shield. Also, an example of how he 'sees' the dangerous world. How his dark place makes him see the world.

I have a mobile phone.

It might go wrong, though. Mum's did.

If it goes wrong, I don't have another.

I won't be able to find help.

I need my old phone back, in case my phone goes wrong and I need to find help.

I diffused any attempts by Leon to talk about tomorrow, or engage with future thoughts. As you can see, they need to be stopped in their tracks.

14th January.
Quiet day. Wonderful beyond your wildest dreams.

I smiled as I typed those words. Minimal stress all throughout the house and family.

My notes tell me there was a disagreement about homework, but, to be honest, so what? I don't remember it.

Leon had a visit from a counsellor today. They talked in a calm, impartial, and productive manner, and we joined in or added our opinions if necessary. I agree, sometimes, about a fresh pair of eyes, or a different point of view joining the situation. Today, it worked. Tomorrow, I might be on the telephone again, complaining.

Leon was advised to make some important decisions, carry out some basic Cognitive Behavioural Therapy (CBT), and push himself for rewards, or the life he wants in the future.

15th January.
We needed lots of patience today, and, I'm glad to say, we both had it. Go Mum and Dad!

There was a strong reluctance to work from Leon. There was a strong reluctance to even think about work.

Due to the visit last night, we were reminded of several techniques for parents to use. We found all of our patience, as I mentioned a moment ago, and ignored any unnecessary conversation or interaction. Sometimes, deliberate or not, children will do anything to stall, or distract, or change the routine they don't agree with.

I worked all day. Mum worked all day. I didn't have any notes about Leon *not* working, so he must have studied.

The grandparents visited this the evening, and they always cheer the house up as well. I believe the social aspect of our family also adds to behaviour here, and not just with Leon. If the evenings, the time after school, and the weekends are monotonous and repetitive, is any change welcomed? Even hoped for?

We do find activities for the children, and take them out when finances allow, but I also know it is something we want and need to improve on.

16th January.
Why can't the simple task of tidying up just be the simple task of tidying up? Why does it have to turn into an hour long discussion?

Yeah, I admit it, I lost my temper by raising my voice, but it happens every time I see Mum upset.

How hard is it to stack a few books in size order, though? To pick up a piece of clothing, or to stop eating sweets in the bedroom? They're not even allowed to eat in the bedroom in the first place!

I told you we don't have many rules here, so why can't

they get a grasp on the most basic ones?

Okay, I love straight lines and a tidy office, but these children have been doing this for years now. Mum and I always end up cleaning the mess in their bedroom. My frustrations, our frustrations, are more than warranted.

I had to pull Leon up on threats. My raised voice scared him, and Sawyer is getting involved, as usual. The threats weren't serious, yet annoying. Said only out of anger.

"You can't touch my stuff, Dad! Stop messing about with my discs!"

"Mate, I'm bloody tidying up for you. What do you want me to do, use my Jedi powers?"

"They're mine! If you touch my stuff, I'll go to your office and mess all your stuff up as well."

Did you notice it? Several lines up? Yes, I typed 'Sawyer is getting involved, as usual.'

Sawyer isn't at school. Sawyer's pain can't decide what it is doing, so neither can Sawyer.

I took Jacob to town. It was a deliberate move to get us away from the tension, and every other emotion, flying around inside the flat. It is horrible to want to be away from your own home, to feel as if you have to get others out for their own happiness. We don't want him to witness any of this. We don't want him to see his brother in a panic. We don't want him to see Leon and Sawyer arguing, and possibly fighting.

Mum watched over Leon while he tidied the bedroom. We often ask ourselves how much is behaviour and how much is the real anxiety. We don't know what is happening inside his mind. It's impossible to, even when he explains the dilemma, or cause.

After we returned home, I walked straight back into the thick of it. I've noticed change is a trigger. Change to routine, change to location, change to any feeling of safety.

We didn't ignore, and we didn't fully engage either. Mum warned Leon he would have to work after three o'clock if he didn't do any study. Of course, this turned into the sum of all fears. He classed it as a detention, but why?

Let me point out a few facts before I continue.

Leon is worried about how annoyed a teacher will have to be to give out a detention.

Leon is worried about getting a detention at school. It wouldn't be through behaviour, it would be through something out of his control. He could forget a book, a piece of homework, the correct set of pens, not being changed in time for a PE lesson. All 'what if I ...?' situations.

Leon has never had a detention.

We need to ask basic questions more often, I believe. We need to cut the thoughts off before they can spread. Try and find the 'core' fear and work on it.

Mum and I agreed to change our minds on this. We ended the study time at three.

When he hasn't been very forthcoming or cooperative, we turn questions towards ourselves. Why should we be understanding and forgiving? The answer is obvious. We're parents. We would rather see them smiling, not crying. Yes, the easy way. Perhaps the incorrect way? Did I mention being a parent was difficult?

Leon's chest hurt for the rest of the day. I told him that all the stress, all the erratic breathing, it will have side effects in a physical sense.

I finally got Leon to sleep between ten and ten-thirty, and I also made a point of speaking to Hugo again. He's at school, he's doing what we want, misbehaviour is at a minimum. However, all the attention is concentrated elsewhere. It's not right. It can't be that way. The message there will be twisted and incorrect.

'If I'm naughty, or cause trouble, Mum and Dad will spend time with me instead.'

No. I don't want the thought to even exist in his mind.

17th January.
I arrived home from Hugo's school run at about nine, and I spoke to him again on the way. He can act casual about such

important topics, yet I know he understood.

Sawyer was getting dressed after a bath, and he told me he was now free of any pain. I'm so glad to hear the news. He has been patient with the recovery, and that isn't a personality trait he is known for. He will turn fourteen in March, and I can see the maturity creeping in. It's being overtaken by snails, but it's still moving forward.

Leon immediately began to complain about pains in his chest, the same as yesterday. He was talking to me about some practice questions, and chapter tests from the textbooks. As soon as he thought about them, the pain started.

"Seriously, mate. Stop overthinking every little detail. Move on to the next section. Come back to the tests on another day."

I can't remember the response, and it isn't in my notes either.

I mentioned an observation of mine to Mum. I am starting to see it all as someone running through narrow streets, perhaps a dense city, being chased. They get cornered, trapped, then find a secret alleyway. The chaser needs to be quick to cut them off, to think ahead and work out where the person will run to next.

Mum returned home with Jacob shortly after eleven o'clock. I forgot to make a note of where they were, although it was probably a parenting group.

Leon changed his behaviour and started to read Harry Potter and the Chamber of Secrets. It's a small win, a step in the right direction, an acceptance of the rules. These changes won't happen overnight, however, I still made it clear we will need to sit down together at the weekend, Mum included, to discuss a new approach. This week proved, without any doubt whatsoever, how much we need to. It didn't work, not as we had planned. It was stressful for all of us, too stressful, not enjoyable or constructive.

Here's a thought. Why did the previous week fail? Forget the anxiety side of it for a moment, or hide it away in the shadows, where it usually lives. Most of our suggestions

were immediately met with resistance, or avoidance?
Why?
Why did they create new worries, or spark old ones?

We want compromise, middle ground, call it what you will, and we must find it.

I spent some time on this, and I love to think. I love to disappear into my own mind, let it all swirl around, then produce answers, possible solutions, reasons, and all the rest.

Even though we have been working with Leon since year four of primary school, I believe we fell into our own complacency. He became safe and adjusted to certain fears, so we believed they weren't going to return. We took a positive view, perhaps one seen through glasses made of hope and relief. Do you know what is really difficult for parents? You already know the answer. Feeling helpless. Admitting you need help. Admitting you were wrong. Not being able to solve a problem.

So, the possible solutions and reasons to come from all of my hours of thought? Use the time we have with Leon to return to the base anxieties. The ones we believed had left him years ago.

Also, we must alter the timetable. We bought those textbooks, then asked him to sit and study for five or six hours per day. His own school timetable worked out to four hours per week for mathematics, English, and science. I matched it. Any chance to learn, even life lessons, will be included in his week. Cooking with Mum. Food technology lesson. Drawing for an hour. Art lesson. Watching an hour of Pride and Prejudice on television. Drama and English combined.

The evening was a great one. Everyone enjoyed themselves with their own interests. We watched John Wick 3. Amazing. Loved it!

18th January.

Quiet morning. Jacob was his usual funny self. I've said it

before, but it really is a superpower. This home wouldn't have as many laughs or smiles if he didn't run around providing them for us all. He can pull anyone out of a bad mood.

We didn't see much of Hugo, which is becoming, or has already become, a family meme.

Sawyer grew more and more annoyed with games on the console, and rage quit a few times. I lost count of the number of F words, and the default volume is eleven. We've warned him about his language on countless occasions, especially if Jacob is near. Still, we're not perfect. We're hypocrites in this respect. Swearing is a choice for me, so I don't add the 'S' word, the 'F' word, or any others unless I am angry, or shouting at sinks, toothpaste lids, empty tea cups that should be full of tea, television remotes playing hide-and-seek, or whatever.

I spoke to Leon about a few things, but also kept it casual. The weekends are still time away from school for him, like any other kid, and I don't have any urge to change the rule.

Nanny and May treated them all to pizza for lunch. She's too generous for her own good sometimes, but, saying no to a nanny is not easy.

There was a lot of thought and conversation about financial matters today.
Paying some of the debts after the will money arrives.
Moving home this year.
Checking finances every month so it is possible to move home this year.

It's all planned for this year. We're proud of our commitment to better finances, to paying the debts. Remember how it all started back in 2018? Yeah, we're also proud of our patience towards the goal. We can do them all. We can.

I said in the introduction about children and patience. How they think in minutes, possibly hours if you're lucky. We have been telling them the reasons for us to sort our finances out, and they do understand, yet there has been minimal complaints about it. I mean, they're not asking every day when we're moving, can they have a takeaway because we paid off more on a bill, or will we buy them more expensive trainers now. We shall make a point of thanking them, and treating them all as well. They deserve it, they really do.

I'm unsure why, yet my notes have another few lines about complacent thoughts towards Leon. Maybe I spoke to Mum again, or something happened to reinforce my ideas. Now it is in our minds, we won't make the same mistake again.

19th January.
I woke up way too early. It was four in the morning, or a time ridiculously close to it. I tried to get back to sleep but my imagination didn't allow it, never usually does. I don't actually mind. I can work and drink my first cup of tea earlier than usual. Win!

A few family members visited for tea and a chat, then a small shopping trip to town followed. Sawyer went out to meet with some of his school friends.

Distraction. It can strike in many forms. Some needed, some unwanted, some forced, and some unnoticed.

Leon has been a distraction. Jacob is two, so he needs our attention. You'll remember Sawyer's emergency surgery from earlier this month. You may also remember his return to school a week ago. Monday was his only day in last week. He was in pain again when he returned home, so we allowed him more time to rest.

This is the distraction I mentioned. We were distracted by Leon, Jacob, Hugo, plus our daily lives, work, and plans. While Sawyer rested, he slipped under our radar.

When he is fine at weekends, enough to bike around town with his friends for hours, he can go back to school, right?

"Maybe. I might be in too much pain tomorrow when I wake up."

"You weren't in pain today."

"Yeah, I know. I might be tomorrow."

Such repetitive conversations can last for hours, and go nowhere.

He also keeps trying to 'advise' Leon about his anxiety.

Do you ever see the same with your children? It's helpful, but it lacks any element of subtlety or tact, even if they don't realise.

In a way, it is just another example of knowing it all. Don't forget, children do something once and the believe they are experts. This is when they sneak off and get medical degrees, psychology degrees, or computer science degrees, but you don't remember them ever doing it. Plus, it only takes a couple of hours to achieve these prestigious academic awards.

I won't say wonderful beyond your wildest dreams. Instead, I'll say amazing, tired, and frustrating.

20th January.

Yeah, Sawyer is vocal about his pain and school, and that is an understatement. Every question we ask, or suggestion we make, is terrible. We need to leave him alone, get out of his face. It makes us believe there's more to it than pain and recovery. Blood from a stone, as they say.

Sawyer carried on after Hugo's school run. He screamed at the top of his lungs. Get out of my fucking room, you don't know what you're talking about, plus a few other colourful requests.

We made it clear, though, while staying calm, that he needs to go back into school tomorrow, or to see the doctor. In our opinion, he needs to ask a few questions and explain what has been happening, in relation to pain and movement, since the surgery.

How can any parent help if they're not allowed to? Impossible job. Impossible. I might go and find the lid off the toothpaste, I feel like swearing at something.

Leon panicked about walking to the local town with me. I got him out of the door after only a short delay. There is DEFINITELY a safety link to his mobile phone and, more importantly, the escape it provides. He wants to ignore the real world and disappear with games or videos.

He overthought everything as we walked up the street, but having a normal chat helped. It was about my work, so unrelated. Another distraction, a forced one, but I genuinely wanted, and valued, his opinion.

After we arrived home, Leon completed an hour of English from the new timetable. We made a chart together, and it allows us to mark off thirty minute study sessions.

Sawyer carried his foul mood through to the evening. All he needed to understand was the importance of getting a note from the doctor. His school have requested one. We're at the point in his absence now when they're asking questions. No, never that simple, is it?

Fuck school. Fuck doctors. I know what they will say to me. You two don't know shit.

Medical degree, yeah?

As you can see, we were all travelling around in frustrated and angry circles. I closed the conversation down and refused to talk any longer.

What would the point be? We all had our opinions, our reasons, yet we couldn't move forward.

I can't remember the reason, the catalyst, but I went into one of my infamous rants during the evening. You all already know how much I wanted this month, this year, this decade, to be different. Is it working out? Exactly.

I ranted about my disappointment, had weak excuses thrown my way, then ended allowance, pocket money, whatever you call it, for good. I introduced a new system at the beginning of the year, but why bother? It hasn't changed one bit. They all receive guaranteed money every week, regardless of behaviour, obeying the rules, their attitude, or how much they help us.

No more.

If they're good, treat us well, act like they've been taught to act, then yeah, I'll review the situation, or give them some money. Otherwise, bollocks. It's not happening.

21st January.

With a little forethought, and some quantum physicist level mathematics, I have tried to predict the size of this book.

Here's the confusing part. I apologise in advance. I'm all for books, reading, the love of literature, but I'm also for everyone being able to afford my work. I will need to split it up, although I don't know yet how the format will be finalised. Every three months? Four? Two books of six months each?

Whatever I decide, I'll list the Kindle versions for a few pounds, and a normal 6.99-8.99 for the paperback, depending on the page count. I suppose I'll know more as the months tick on.

Sawyer is off school, *again*.

Insert any emoji here relating to annoyance.

As discussed, we booked him an appointment with the doctor, and he agreed. Then, after a relaxing bath, very suddenly, the pain disappeared.

Of course, *we* were shouted at for being annoyed and confused at the constant change to his pain. *We* were overreacting. *We* needed to calm down. Whatever.

Leon told me some personal thoughts tonight, so I'm camping out in the front room with him. It's a late night chat, boys night! Where's the beer? Wait, Leon is too young, so where's *my* beer?

We do this at home when there are illnesses, bad nightmares, or similar. Yes, it is difficult to sleep without Mum, and she feels the same.

When Hugo suffered his seizure, all of us were in there! We dragged so many mattresses through, then placed them next to each other until it fit. A great memory to come from a bad experience.

Bob and Ratbag. Remember those names. I may return to them.

We spoke to Hugo again. He's such a cool kid, and we keep telling him so. We know, as I said earlier, we *must* share our time and attention, no matter what else is happening. It can be the new Hugo meme. Instead of seeing him for two minutes between games of football on his console, we will seek him out and make time to check in.

22nd January.
We had an impromptu conversation with a counsellor this morning. It was about, well, something. We needed to hear their view, their interpretation of a specific situation. They broke it down for us, gave specific advice. Some of it was, and will be, quite easy. Some of it was, and will be, extremely difficult. All of the words were useful. I reminded the counsellor of my disappointment and anger during the telephone call on the 13th. Again, it was explained that their words were not meant in such context. They needed to be said, though.

I just scrolled back to the 13th. I suppose, in its easiest form, or one of its easiest forms, I'm saying be mindful of your behaviour and actions. They will be seen by the child or children, heard, remembered, copied, overthought, taken the wrong way, even worried about.
None of us want to add to the problem, or problems, do we?

I had already noticed a pattern with Leon, maybe a few patterns, subconscious or not. You see, he isn't the type to scam or cheat, not if he knows it will cause trouble. The lie will eat away at him. Anyway, the pattern, or patterns. As soon as work is mentioned, school work, or not what he wants to do, the panic sets in. He's evolved again, although I believe he has reached a peak. He can't go further. Only forward and better.

The realisation of such patterns, plus the advice, led us to change our behaviour today. Firstly, we told Leon how much time he was permitted to talk to us for. There have been hours of repetition with this condition, as you know from reading the previous entries. The same words and sentences are spoken, over and over.

Over and over.

Over and over.

We made it clear he will not be able to enjoy himself at break, lunch, or straight after school hours, not unless he earns it first. Complacency is also an enemy. Busy parents can, *and will*, take their eyes off the situation, unintentionally, and the child won't usually mention it.

Leon was prescribed a calming medicine back in September, I think I have already mentioned it, so we will use it on a regular basis now. My thought here is prevention. Prevention management, which is a term I just typed, although I doubt I'll use it again. It's too professional and medical.

It was a long, long, very long, day. Never underestimate the strength of a child. I'm not talking about physical here, but their mental resolve. It's impressive. Leon fought back against all the changes, all the new rules, even our own changes in attitude.

He wasn't allowed to do what he wanted to do, when he wanted to do it. He wanted long and repetitive conversations, time with us to change the routine. He wanted online study, not the textbooks. We wouldn't allow it. Every aspect of the patterns presented themselves, in full power glory.

He eventually wore himself out, physically, and with the help of calming medicine.

Yes, this is tough, heartbreaking, soul destroying, and it will be tough, heartbreaking, and soul destroying for a while yet. Speaking again about mental resolve, I hope we have enough to continue.

We made a decision today and spoke to the other children about it. They need to understand how important it is only *we* deal with issues, not them. We do not want them getting involved. No advice, no discussion, and no unnecessary conversation.

Do you think they'll listen? Yeah, I'm dubious about the question as well.

23rd January.

Sawyer returned to school! Add the sound effect of an audience clapping and cheering again! Haha!

After arranging appointments with the doctor, cancelling them, warning him about the notes school requested for his absences, it was about time. I have a feeling it will be twisted and we'll become 'pushy parents' in future weeks or months.

Jacob has a slight cold, but he is going out with Mum this morning to a playgroup. They used to be regulars, but Christmas is busy, life with four children is busy, and plans suffer occasionally.

They do deserve a break. They really deserve to get away for a while. You may have already noticed we don't have much of a social life. Yeah, we know. We're working on it.

Leon is in a great mood this morning. He's engrossed in school work, which is more than helpful. I've needed some quiet times, and an 'empty' flat for parts of my work. I used the time wisely and recorded videos and voice notes, then updated social media for a couple of hours.

Leon and I met with Mum and Jacob at the playgroup. He briefly saw one of his school teachers, but didn't talk to her much. She is one of the understanding ones, so knows about the anxiety, *and* everything that goes with it.

I worked constantly for the afternoon, Mum did as well, and Leon studied.

Leon and Hugo are members of a local youth club, and attended for a couple of hours this evening.

Leon told me he enjoyed it, even though I wasn't sure if he would even want to socialise, and Hugo can be reluctant to go on his own.

This was a great day. It is so much easier when stress doesn't play a part.

24th January.

Straight to work this morning. I had to fix a paper jam in the printer. Haha!

Leon said he felt ill, like Jacob. I wasn't sure if it was completely true, and I felt a slight tinge of guilt for questioning it. Compromise is useful. Have I told you before about the illness rules here? Well, in regards to school, unless they're contagious, or throwing up, they go in. Yes, if we get a telephone call from the school nurse, we do as suggested, but we stick to it.

"Okay, you do half hour of study, then we will see how you feel."

Half an hour later, Leon ended up in bed. The system works. Winky face.

Some work is planned for the flat. Or, they'll offer us a 3 or 4 bedroom. As I type this in the notes, an email arrives.

Yeah, so, we're *slightly* behind on the rent. The balance needs clearing for three consecutive months. We also need to place a new guarantor on file, then we're allowed to look at bigger properties.

Quiet evening, however, I let a few thoughts whirl around. Let me explain.

I think it's time to close the self-employed aspect and return to work. It all links in with our situation, and how I sometimes believe I am making it worse. I've already mentioned this, back on the 6th of January, but it always brings up a conflict. I can't believe money will change so many aspects of life. I also strongly believe a change in lifestyle will. One of the ways to achieve the change, unfortunately, is with more money.

Watch this space, yeah?

25th January.

Straight to work this morning, as soon as I had finished my first tea. This book, others, edits, the usual really. It is therapeutic, as I mentioned earlier, and upsetting, as I also mentioned.

Do you know the most helpful part?

Seeing what I, or we, did in certain situations. Seeing what worked, what failed, and what can be improved on.

Jacob slept well, despite the blocked nose from his cold, and Leon has a birthday party later today. Guess where? The games console maze from the 5th of January.

We want this to be a great, wonderful beyond your wildest dreams, kind of day.
Leon needs it.
We all need it.

He doesn't have all the wanted guests attending, because he couldn't get into school to hand out the invites.

We tried to encourage him, we really did. Our approach and mentality towards it was to weigh up the reward for effort and bravery.

"If you go to school, you can hand out the invites. Then, your friends will be there as well."

Or similar words.

There will still be enough friends and family present, and they will be those who matter, which is also important.

Nanny and May visited today as usual. Their few hours here are always such a great laugh, and Jacob was making them smile.

"Yeah, Nanny. My arty!"

"Your party?"

"Yeah, my arty."

As you can tell, he is at the stage where a lot of 'things' are his. His birthday. His party. His chair. His crisps.

Nanny doesn't have any news or gossip from the old neighbourhood, which we talk about sometimes. It is always interesting to see and hear about how everyone has grown up. Some are still local, some are on the other side of the world.

The afternoon was a slow and quiet one, probably because we are waiting for the party later. Yes, we are all impatient, even the 'usually patient' adults.

Here's a strange note to add, linked to the games

console maze. Sawyer's birthday party last year was also held at the same place. I was inside for five to ten minutes before I received a telephone call. A telephone call I had both dreaded and expected.

I visited V in hospital that morning, although she didn't know I was there. Sedation, antibiotics, lack of strength, there are a few reasons why she wasn't conscious.

On the telephone call, I was informed that one of the many doctors treating V wanted everyone involved to get there and say our final words to her. As you may remember from the introduction, that is exactly what happened.

Leon's party was amazing. He really enjoyed himself, and desperately needed the break. The break from his own thoughts, from this house, from the terrible few weeks he has had. Yes, not everyone he wanted was there, like I said earlier, but enough. He smiled, laughed, and ate way too much pizza and sweets.

That's all we wanted to see today.

It's only eight in the evening and I am ready for bed! I've been doing this for over a decade, I mean birthday parties for the children, and it is tiring.

It was great to catch up with some friends, geek about on games for a couple of hours, and smile ourselves. Oh, and don't forget the massive chocolate cake. Awesome!

26th January.

Apparently, Hugo and Leon stayed up talking until nearly two in the morning. They do this at weekends a lot. Sometimes, it's the 'all night challenge', sometimes they simply forget to look at a clock or watch. It explained their reluctance to get out of bed today.

One of Leon's friends, very close, but now at another senior school, might be coming over for a few hours today. He was at the party last night and they always have a laugh together. Nine years of solid friendship is all the proof needed of a close bond.

I remember those days, do you? The school friends you couldn't wait to see again? Very cool. If it was a school day, you couldn't wait until the next morning, if it was a weekend, you'd spend the whole of Monday morning telling each other stories.

"You two! Stop talking and get on with your work!"

I can hear teachers of the past saying those words right now.

All the children went out on their bikes, except Hugo. He's still a bit too young, and not yet a confident enough rider. We get some backlash for saying it, but we believe it's the correct decision in the long run. Also, there is a slight element of 'parent trust' involved. Sawyer and Leon are older, and are allowed further. Children can make … interesting decisions sometimes. We don't want Hugo taken miles away, just because his older brothers have suggested it, and he feels there is no other choice.

They all had lots of fun as far as I was told. Leon did hurt his back, a muscle strain in my opinion, so nothing serious.

Pizza again for dinner, but they didn't complain. I can't eat pizza because I switched to soya only a few years back. Normal dairy was causing too much discomfort, so I'm jealous. I miss pizza!

Mum is ill with a cold, and that is all she needs right now. I'll look after her, although she doesn't need me to. I've told you before how strong she is, right?

Here's something funny. I joke, a lot. If I'm ill, I joke with Mum, or tease her, or wind her up.

"It makes me feel better. Laughter is the best medicine, you know that."

I also use the same if Mum is ill. Sometimes she laughs, sometimes she rolls her eyes and calls me a 'meanie'.

Leon crashed early, exhausted from the weekend and late nights.

I had to chat with Hugo because of a nightmare,

made worse because his brothers were asleep. Scary is even scarier when you are alone, I get that.

An advert came up during a Youtube video for a horror movie, and he didn't look away fast enough. I thought this was meant to be changing at the beginning of the year? Do you remember reading about it? The COPPA ruling? New laws and regulations were put in place for children and their online viewing. I mean, the answer is simple enough. Hugo was watching a video from a familiar channel, yet it hadn't been classed as only for kids. It doesn't prove any innocence or blame. It proves the new rules and laws aren't very effective at all.

27th January.

I am absolutely shattered! I didn't sleep last night until nearly two in the morning, but I don't remember there being a reason.

School couldn't open for Sawyer, so he was off again. A water main burst somewhere further past town. Sixteen schools were closed, and thousands of homes went without running water. It was classed as a serious incident after only a short time.

I'm nervous about the absence, though. Sawyer's patience with Leon is worth a couple of minutes, maybe less.

Mum and Jacob went to town. They needed to buy a few presents and supplies for Leon's birthday later this week.

Now, I don't know exactly which part of all this situation sparks my impatience, frustration, or anger, but I wasn't calm today. I didn't want hours of stress. I wanted to work, and I wanted Leon to accept he was too, without questions or unnecessary conversation.

He immediately gave me trouble. He didn't want to pick up any of the textbooks. He was tired. He wanted a bit of a rest, then he'd be fine.

I raised my voice. "Quiet!"

He was right behind me, breathing erratically, and I was *trying* to work. All the children forget, too easily, I am one person, running a business.

Sometimes, raising my voice works. The children realise they've stepped over a line, and it is all sorted and over within minutes. Today, Leon flew towards an anxious extreme. I paid no attention, though. Patterns, right? I may have been wrong, I may have interpreted the scene incorrectly, but I wasn't prepared to give any of my time.

Mum bought an anxiety workbook in town, one we had already researched. Leon loved it from the moment he saw it. Do such actions prove how much he wants to understand, control, and manage all his worries?

The mind fascinates me so much. I studied psychology for a degree several years ago, with the Open University. If any of you are wondering about study later in life, no matter your age, current career, even financial situation, go and take a look. I recommend it, and I will return to study at some point in the future. Unfortunately, I never completed my full degree, yet I still hope to do so.

Leon's school attendance staff visited again for a brief conversation. A meeting was booked, and shortly after we received a very encouraging and understanding email. We are presuming a reduced timetable will be offered as an initial step, based on our own knowledge of the process. However, Mum is not going to leave without *all* the answers to *all* the questions.

How will it work if he can't even get the school uniform on?

What if he can't get in to school on a planned day?

Who will be there to assist him if we are not?

Are the people, or, is the person named above qualified in child psychology?

That's strange. I typed 'plus more' in my notes. Guess what? My mind has gone blank.

It wasn't easy for Sawyer to stay quiet about today's events, but he did listen when I asked him to. As I said earlier, he has no patience and likes to dish out advice.

After dinner, we chatted to Leon. I mean, we had no choice in the matter. Let me expand on this.

There are many different routes to take, and, as this book demonstrates, they aren't always successful. We have thought of using others, or mixtures of several. We agreed sticking to one method would be less confusing for all concerned. Also, Leon's symptoms and behaviour aren't following a route. They are all random, spontaneous, unexpected, and constantly changing.

Since the 7th of January, we have been understanding, accommodating, and mostly calm. Yes, as many of you have already probably screamed at the Kindle screen, or pages of the book, we could have acted differently. You may have seen something obvious we've missed.

We could have walked him to school and got him in. We could have disassociated ourselves with the 'system' and sought private medical advice. We could have given up and let fate take its course. We could have pulled him out of school, checked the bank accounts, then paid for home tutors.

I'm ranting again. The reason we spoke to Leon was because, despite all of our help and understanding, he isn't happy. I'm not talking about conducting a study here, or anything like that.

Unhappy children versus happy ones, and the result for education and learning. It sounds interesting, but no.

I'm talking about base level, core happiness.

If all of our understanding, accommodating, and mostly calm tactics aren't working, what does he actually want? Why does he still put up walls and barriers? Why isn't our system working?

Answers weren't found, and when we decided to take back some of the time from earlier, while he wasn't studying due to his tired reluctance, he grew angry.

"We've decided you can't use your mobile phone, for anything, until you go through to the bedroom later. You can have it to help you sleep. That's it, though. It's only fair."

Anger followed, plus lots of apologies. We kept calm.

We talked about the reasons for our decision and got him through.

Before bed, he wrote us both a lovely letter. It thanked us for staying with him, he apologised again for the bad behaviour, and he told us how much we are helping him. It was an exercise straight out of new anxiety workbook. I won't copy any of it in, it's too personal.

I can tell you we both smiled.

Hugo needed me. He wasn't specific on the reason or reasons, he simply needed me. I wanted to know why, although it doesn't take a genius to work it out. Everyone in the family is dealing with the current situation in their own way, but it isn't healthy. Our home is sick of it. We must stay strong, together.

I might go to the library this week and work there for a couple of days. I definitely want to catch up on the notes for this book. If too much time passes between those and writing, plus edits, I could lose vital information. This is about emotions, about the moment. There's no way I will be able to remember all of them.

I managed ten minutes in bed before the phone rang. My mum had hurt her thumb, and it worried her enough to call me. I got dressed, telephoned for a taxi, then went over.

I think I reassured her by simply being there. She knew it wasn't serious, but she had to hear those words from someone else. It wasn't broken, so I told her to try and get some sleep.

I crashed on her sofa, eventually, at close to two in the morning.

28th January.
Woke up at about seven. It was a strange flashback to see the house I grew up in as I opened my eyes, yet a pleasant one. Well, a great one, if I'm honest. I have some awesome memories of that place, and time in my life. I mentioned that on the 9th.

I decided to stay with my mum today, until after she had seen a doctor.

Hugo sent me a few texts from home, before he left for school. Remember when he needed me yesterday? Yeah, it was exactly what I thought, about helping Leon. It is rippling, as I mentioned on the 6th. I will speak to him later and see a way forward, *without* placing too much worry or responsibility on his shoulders. He is nine, as you know. These children need to be children, not children taking on adult thoughts. There will be a compromise, somewhere.

My mum returned from the doctor, and all is fine. It is most likely tendon damage, hence the problems with any movement of her thumb. She told me it could be a couple of weeks until full recovery, though, and possibly return visits. If she needs me, or the rest of the family, we will be there to help.

I chatted, worked hard with the time I had available, then called a taxi home. My other sister, we can call her Jasmine, returns from work later in the afternoon, so she will find out about the adventures then, and probably laugh at the ludicrous nature of it all. It's our way. We laugh as soon as we can.

I worked again at home for a while, then left for Hugo's school run. I want to talk to him about this morning, and update him about Nanny as well. I wasn't there when they woke up, and even though it sounds like a small change, it is very unusual for us as a family.

I managed to talk briefly about Leon on the way home. It's a short journey of fifteen minutes, or close to it. Hugo wants to help, but he also said it's always in his head, distracting him, even in lessons. We will decide on the way forward, together, or involve the school for assistance. They are very helpful.

Apart from Sawyer seeming to have a problem with EVERYTHING Hugo did or said during dinner, there were no other worries. I'm hoping for a quiet and early night. I need it after my two late ones, and I'm starting to feel the tiredness mentally and physically. Of course, I could receive another telephone call about a sore thumb at any point.

Leon is excited for his birthday tomorrow. He worked without any stress today. Now, is it because of me? Is some of the behaviour and consequent action because I'm at home, working? It has been mentioned in the past, in a detrimental, please-give-it-some-serious-thought sense. I am at home, I represent safety, and I can stay inside the house. Why can't he? Why can't he do the same as Dad?

I see the point and can agree, but I also see a few other sides to it, and disagree. Also, most importantly, I can't afford an office space at the moment.

Mum is ill with her cold, but we managed a couple of hours of television before bed.

29th January.
Hours of work this morning, and I am proud of myself for all of it. I worked on this book, other books, new projects, side projects, marketing, and kept pushing. I want at least one other book out this year, as well as these. I still believe it will be split up into four parts.

I don't care about today. Wait, that could be too easily misunderstood. Leon turns twelve, so, no matter what, I *will make* this brilliant and stress free. For him. For everyone. I will look back at today, along with everybody else, and remember it in a positive way.

Here is a random question for you. Have you ever had such a bad day, for whatever reason, you wrote the whole thing off as if it never happened?

I have. There were big 'X' marks on old calendars. Those days when it never stopped. It couldn't be forgotten, forgiven, it dragged on, or it kept resurfacing and bringing the anger or sadness back?

I ask because I am so determined for Leon's birthday, I have 'tweaked' the above method. I will mark a big tick, or a heart, or a scribbled star on today. *If* anything even tries to ruin the special time, dares to, I will bounce it off my shield and chase it away.

On the way home, just before we bought the birthday takeaway, Mum received a telephone call from Leon's school. They spoke about a possible solution called 'home tuition'. It does exactly what it says on the tin, although, the library, or a classroom could also be locations. The basics would be periods with a tutor, sitting and learning from the current curriculum. My instincts crossed my fingers. I want it accepted.

Nanny is doing okay, although there is still no movement in her thumb. She also told me she keeps forgetting and carrying on with her daily routine. Want to try it for yourself? It's fine, we won't be offended, haha!

Okay, hold your thumb straight, both joints.

Done it?

Off you go. Have fun.

Nanny and Grandad visited this evening with more presents for Leon. The whole family smiled, laughed, and joked. Once again, moments made of solid gold.

30th January.
Leon and Mum watched Hugo in a school play today. He loves drama class, acting, and has performed in many plays at school.

I should have a code in these books. Instead of repeating myself every day, or couple of days, I could type 'Code R' for 'Resistance to study'. 'Code P' for 'Panic.'

Why has it taken me a month to think of that? Of course, the downside is I want to talk about the situations, to try and understand or explain why they're happening in the first place, not just type them away in a couple of words.

'Code R'. 'Code R!'.

Sounds a bit dramatic. Yeah, we'll see.

Leon also worked on the anxiety book, the one he *will* touch, some calming exercises, and completed an hour of online study.

I churned out over three thousand words this morning, so I am pleased. Ecstatic. I love it when the words flow so fast, and my brain is ticking over. My poor fingers can't keep up the pace.

Leon's afternoon was productive and quiet, but still not filled with enough study, not in my opinion. Another question for all, and myself. How do I know what is enough? As I described at the beginning of the month, I follow the school timetable, so I'm confident.

Youth club tonight for Leon and Hugo, and all the children present watched Wonder. It prepares them all for a future session on bullying, friendship, friendship despite someone being different, and other issues they will face through life.

Home for a relaxing evening. Mum felt ill, although the doctor has prescribed her some medication. Her symptoms should start to ease soon, I hope.

I checked my email account and found one from a known solicitors office. Formal letters are going to be sent very soon. The will money is almost ready to release, once the final paperwork is prepared.

I became two different people. I'm pissed off. I'm angry again. I'm upset, *again*. I am also relieved, looking forward to paying off a couple of debts, and pleased we can all, finally, move on from last year.

Mum told me to focus on the positives, even though she knows I don't need reminding. She knows the shield will work.

All in all, a normal day. No, wait, normal can be confused with my 'normal' list in the introduction. Peaceful, relaxing, a few easily solved issues, and happiness.

Here's an interesting point, though, and I am unsure why it is in the notes. 'If they look and act happy, does it mean they are?'

I must have seen someone smile, laugh, or similar, but questioned what was really going on inside. Or, was it about my own behaviour?

The day ended with television and tea.

31st January.

Leon worked on a few different subjects, although his eyes were on a delivery today. He ordered a musical instrument with his birthday money, and it's almost taken over his entire focus. Excitement, anticipation, the dreaded impatience as well. Seriously, I don't remember inviting Impatience to live here, so why does it?

Leon has a natural talent in regards to music. Reading sheet music is still difficult, and it will take time and dedication, but ask him to remember a tune, let him listen a few times, and it's there, in his mind forever. Music is also a phenomenal form of therapy, so we're interested to see where it all leads.

Mum did a favour for a friend today, so we had two other children here for a couple of hours. Loads of fun, screaming fun, shouting fun, chasing fun … you get the idea. Sharing wasn't amazing, however, they're young. Jacob and Mum loved it. She is feeling better now, thankfully, so all the extra noise didn't mess with her head.

The evening saw a slight moan about allowance money from Sawyer. My reasons were questioned and twisted. I saw it as an attempt to make me the bad guy, to make me wrong, to make me believe I made a terrible decision. I didn't get involved or explain myself. I'm going to stick to my plan and see where it goes, for now. I also know I may change my mind in a few weeks, or months, or whatever, and call myself stupid for even thinking of it in the first place.

Wow! An entire month already? Really? I'm so glad I committed to this project. It is definitely therapeutic, although, when I have to relieve the memories of terrible moments or days, it brings the raw sadness back.

It has also shown me how much I need to find those positives, and how well we're actually coping, regardless of how much the super-busy, tea-spilling Universe sends our way.

I won't type out a long 'review', but a short visit back through the month can't hurt. Imagine it as a meeting with your manager. Yeah, you're called in, sat down, a big file with your name on the front is open on the desk.

I just went through the partially edited section. It runs from the 1st to the 21st. Thirteen days mention 'wonderful beyond your wildest dreams'. Of course, it's an irrelevant number or statistic. Time for a copy and paste!

'When you weigh it all up, when you list the pros against the cons, what are you really left with? I suppose this is an important point which I will return to many times in the book. This is also how I look at the world. Every single day. Every single day.

If the good is always somewhere, how powerful can the bad ever actually become? Yes, I know, that sounds like such a cliché, an extremely annoying one, however, if you can find positives, they will always help you. Here's another annoying cliché. The good and positive, no matter how small or seemingly insignificant, provide you with a protective shield. They are your barrier, built to keep all the bad and upsetting away. The photo of you and your partner which brings back a special memory, a song, shooting the enemy on a computer game, a film, a show on television, your kid laughing or calling your name when you get home.'

"Hi, Blake."

"Hi … erm … manager person? We've never met. I literally just made you up, so you don't have a name yet. Sorry. I'll sort it out for our next meeting."

"Shall we get to it, then?"

"Do we need to? I can't see the point, if I'm honest."

"You can't see the point?"

"No."

"You realise what this is, Blake? This is a monthly review. Your actions, decisions, failures, and triumphs. We need to discuss all of them."

"We're working on it, hour by hour, day by day. That's, you know, life. I know it isn't 'perfect', whatever that means, but I never expected it to be that way."

"I see."

"So, shall I go back to work?"

"Yes, Blake, I suppose you should. Tell me, before you leave, do you know what you need to work on? Do you know where you need to make improvements?"

"Yes. I know."

So, the good is always there, as I said a few hundred words ago, even if I have to search until the final second in a day to find it.

Yes, we are dealing with some serious issues right now, but, it is part of the 'job'. That is the essence of it, the essence of parenthood. What happens on the dark days? What happens when the arguments strike?

As you can see from the previous month, I have made some good choices, some great ones, some bad ones, and some downright horrendous ones. My actions have been controlled by calm, anger, impatience, tolerance, confusion and understanding. Plus, we can't forget instinct. Those split second decisions. You hope they're going to be correct, you hope they will help.

I must always use, and trust, in the shield.

I must keep the shield strong. I will use any positive to build it.

I must never turn to the Dark Side. Anger will not prevail. Ever.

I am surrounded by positives, every second of my life. My life is challenging, yes, but I smile, laugh, tell jokes, and dance. There is love in my family, in my life, so much of it.

We will get through any and all problems. We will. All of them. I have to believe it as a fact, an unquestionable truth.

See you all in the next book! Smiley face.

AN 'EXTRA' UNTITLED BOOK ABOUT PARENTING.

February & March

Introduction

Welcome back, readers! How are you? I hope you have all found your own 'wonderful beyond your wildest dreams', or are heading along the right path to do so?

This introduction will be shorter than at the beginning of January. Well, it should be, shouldn't it?

In the real world, these introductory notes were taken on the 21st of February, and it is the 24th of February today. Not long until the end of the month. Not long until March! Maybe time is flying along, unnoticed? I mention later how these books are intense and often take up entire days of work, ten plus hours, in the blink of an eye. I have already learnt being a diarist is definitely a strong commitment, and not one to be entered into lightly.

The children have just finished a half-term off school, and we all SURVIVED! Laughing emoji. Stick in lots of heart emojis as well, because I'm like that. Soft and all for the emotions.

Memory tells me February was calmer, easier, and quieter. We'll all find out if that was actually true, or am I only focusing on the wonderful? Did I use my shield so much I can't remember the bad, or refuse to remember it?

We paid a few debts, some bills as well, so, in that regard, life is moving forward. Life is heading in a positive direction.

No, we *still* haven't made it out for a date, just the two of us.

We will.

We will.

Will we?

As you will read soon, I decided to release January on its own. I wanted it out. I wanted it published. This project may break my heart at times, but it also excites me, it has grabbed my attention. Those words sound strange, seeing as it is about me and the family. Of course it will grab my attention. However, it also forces me to look at myself, my behaviour, my actions, and my choices. I *will* act differently because of this.

Every single day?

Every month?

Not until the 31st of December, when I complete the whole year?

I'm afraid I can't answer.

This book will run until the end of March, minimum. I have a rough outline and plan. I'm also thinking ahead to the paperback versions as well.

Right, back to the here and now. I know what I want to change for this book. I know what I need to include, and a main part of that is the wonderful beyond your wildest dreams. Okay, I wrote about all those times in January, however, why was it such a time, or a day? Why? I must shout about all the reasons in CAPITAL letters. Or **bold.** Or **BOTH.** All the reasons are important, so they need to be here.

Let's get to it. I'll see you at the end of each month for a chat with the management team. We met one in January, but there are more now. It is like The Apprentice, Dragon's Den, or an episode of Britain's Got Talent. I'll even give them names this time, as promised. Ridiculous or unusual names? Of course!

An idea sparked as I wrote the previous sentence. I do so love it when that happens.

Do I include a child on the team? Do I include a balanced opinion? A child's view of the situations?

Interesting questions. I'll give them some thought.

Chapter two

February

1st February.
Oh my days, I haven't even had a cup of tea yet. This is a serious situation! I'll sort one, then carry on making notes if I need to.

I'm back. I drank the first cup of tea, then immediately made another. So, as I said, I got up earlier, sat down in the office, then started writing the ending for yesterday. I have absolutely no idea why.
Dedication? Yes, of course, I'm dedicated, that's the reason. Dedication without tea, though? Ridiculous! Riddikulus! Take your pick.

Guess what? I have nothing stressful, or negative, or upsetting to write about today. Nothing at all. Can I get a high-five? Awesome!

We visited town early, so we could be back in time for Nanny and May's visit.

In town, I bought a robot. At home, I built a robot. Then, we all laughed and played with a robot.

Nanny treated us to a takeaway dinner, again. She is too generous. I hope I can say the same when I reach her age. I'd love to be remembered in such a way.

"Blake? Oh, he's such a great guy. Always helpful, always trying to help."

The first day of a new month and I'm already using copy and paste.

All I have to say is modern parenting can be amazing, difficult, challenging, beautiful, stressful, frustrating, loving, upsetting, or, as it should be, wonderful beyond your wildest dreams.

2nd February.

Some of Mum's family visited earlier this morning. There were a few pieces of gossip to hear, news, laughs, and some serious adult conversation as well. It's the usual.

Sawyer went out with some of his friends. In all honesty, he keeps his social life private, and his school is further than what I would class as 'local', so we don't know many of them. We do know he enjoys himself, and the break from a monotonous, mundane weekend.

Hugo was injured a couple of times during play this morning. Well, injured is the incorrect term. Children playing together will inevitably get a bump here and there. He got annoyed, more than usual, because he hadn't got over the first before the second happened, *and* he wanted to be left alone. Being alone, or even finding a place to be, is not easy in this flat. There is nowhere to go!

In the end, he sat behind Jacob's pushchair, in a corner by the front door! Haha!

A shopping trip followed, yet not to town. I know, shocking, right? No, we went the other way today. Such rebels! Haha!

During the times when I am out with Mum, we talk about anything and everything. Today, I bored her … wait, I mean I discussed work ideas with her. Haha!

If I try to carry out every plan, and release every book, I'm going to have a busy year, believe me.

We saw some old friends at the supermarket, so we stopped for a quick chat. We haven't seen as much of them as we used to, not since their daughter started senior school. It's a shame because our kids all grew up together. Every morning and afternoon we would chat in the school playground, there were parties as well, sports days, and school events. Mum arranged a catch up for a couple of weeks time.

Here's a thought. Mum and I found our way towards it while we were walking home.

In the first book, on the 29th of January, I wrote about home tuition, offered by the school. In case there is any confusion, it also falls under the title of medical tuition. I believe it is designed for children who are going to be out of school for a certain period of time. The reason could be anything covered by the 'medical' title. For example, a prolonged stay in hospital, or at home, due to surgery, or long term illness.

The thought we found our way to? What happens if the proposal from school *doesn't* work out? Then what?

We've realised, as parents, any and all the news you receive has to go through different organisations, or professionals, before you can even begin to class it as good or bad, or even completely disappointing. They seem to decide this for you as well, sometimes. An amazing idea to you might be a terrible one to these organisations or professionals, and vice versa.

All the news can also be confusing because of this, and by that I mean you don't know if you are making the correct decision about it. Instinct makes you smile, whereas professional advice, or your own experiences or knowledge, will cause hours of overthought.

Not a great situation, is it? Hopes inevitably rise, only to hang unsecured, unsure if they're going to fall.

Leon became agitated as we spoke of Monday, but we got him calm and he distracted himself with medicine and

YouTube. I think I will work on some of my own CBT ideas tomorrow, for him.

Sawyer 'helped' as well. Can you hear my sighs?

I didn't mean to sound sarcastic or condescending, I promise. It is simply frustrating at times, and so very repetitive.

Leon listened to about an hour of advice. It included encouragement, some scare tactics for want of a better phrase, questions he could not answer, and promises he will not be able to keep.

None of it made a difference, and, even though I am being presumptuous, I don't believe any of it will make a difference.

Of course, we pointed this out after thirty seconds, but Sawyer carried on. He knows best. We're not doing it properly, so he has no choice but to step in.

Can you hear my eyes rolling over the sound of my sighs?

3rd February.
Mum and Jacob went out for a few hours, to town. My notes don't tell me why.

Hugo and Sawyer are at school, so I'm here with Leon. I'm ready to tackle some issues with him. I'm more than ready. I don't expect success, not for a second, but it all has to start at some point, right?
I have a couple of hours of work to complete first, then a few housework chores.

Okay, up there, a few lines ago, plus an entry from yesterday as well.

'I don't expect success, not for a second ...'

'I think I will work on some of my own CBT ideas tomorrow, for him.'

Guess what? I *did* expect success, even if I didn't realise. I didn't see it going wrong. I ... am so tired. At this exact moment, I actually don't know where to turn next. During times like this, I love my shield.

Leon has grown to detest the textbooks, the ones we bought on the 9th of January. There is also another pressing issue I wanted to start working through, one I won't elaborate on. I'll call it … vegetable soup.

I thought I could break it down into steps, as I have learnt from therapists in the past, and work on overcoming those steps one by one.

Have you ever heard of neuroplasticity?

It sounds like the storyline for a science fiction novel, yet it is very real and very true. I have studied the topic in some depth, during my psychology degree.

Okay, here is the somewhat complicated, science fiction plot I mentioned. Humans can 'rewire' their own brains, through the use of thoughts and actions.

Yeah, I know. Amazing, right?

The basis has been used widely in medical fields, for a variety of purposes, and it has benefitted many people.

Let's say, for example, a person is afraid of … lilac underpants … with white dots on them.

I'll stick a disclaimer in here straight away. I am no expert. This is just for explanation purposes. It's also rather ludicrous because lilac underpants with white dots on them sound AMAZING! FABULOUS!

Right, back to the serious stuff. Over the course of, say, a month, the person will slowly work towards loving the underpants. They will use exposure techniques, and push themselves further day by day. They will unwire the fear, and make a new 'wire'. This new wire will tell their brain they love the pants. This new wire will have NOTHING to do with fear.

I know I have used this technique before, not with pants, (sad face) but with my own fears and worries.

I'll break down, briefly, how I planned to help Leon.
He hates the textbooks.

He hates the idea of vegetable soup. (Remember, that is a code for something else. It's back up the page somewhere, in case you missed it.)

A few minutes with the textbooks, more if he can, then take a break. Repeat the simple process, until comfortable. I aimed to use the same for the vegetable soup.

My 'amazing' idea ruined the entire morning. I can't believe I was so naïve, so focused. I never thought of failure. I was also guilty. I had ruined Leon's morning, made him anxious, upset, and brought feelings of failure onto his shoulders.

I spoke to Mum about the way forward. A possible NEW way forward. It seems to be one of the only topics we discuss at the moment, and that is such a sad way to live.

I've mentioned the void already. The strange place parents travel to while meetings and appointments are made, dates set, and letters printed. I've also mentioned that as qualified as these people are, they do not live in our home on a daily basis. They do not live through what we live through.

Okay, this provides them with impartiality, and their skill often relies on such, but, to the parents, it doesn't ease any worries, fears, or anxiety.

We have already put a lot of faith and blind belief in Leon's counselling being successful. We are always advised to allow the process to run its course, to be patient, to listen to advice no matter how difficult it is to hear. We are also told to stay calm around the child, or children. To control all of our emotions, so they don't transfer, or influence behaviour.

What if, and I am asking this because I discussed it with Mum today, you've reached a point where it is impossible to follow any advice? You're at your limit. You can't keep it in any longer. Your only concern is to bring the mood of the family back towards happiness. You can't stand the tension, so you have to look at the larger picture, the future.

I apologise if I have given any of you a headache.

The problem I see with all the patience, waiting, and trying to act a certain way? What if it keeps getting worse?

I'm talking about the entire family when I ask the question. What if we *all* reach our limits?

By the time any help arrives, Leon will be one small part of a much larger problem.

The system, eh? You really want to trust it. You really, really, do.

Also, as a short addition, here's a personal thought. When I had counselling many years ago, I had six hours. One hour per week for six weeks. When we spend more than that with Leon in a single day, trying to help, and not always finding it successful, it explains why we have so much difficulty believing their methods will bring forth any improvement.

All quiet for the evening. Why can't it be like this during the day? The relief definitely falls after three o'clock in the afternoon, especially for Leon. I do wish he wasn't agitated, that it wasn't so difficult for him to enjoy the normal parts of a day.

I have an earache, and feel as if a cold is creeping in. Not surprising, if you think about it. Such stress will eventually start producing physical symptoms as well, unfortunately.

4th February.

Hugo went to see a doctor before school this morning. He complained about a pain in his back, after Sunday's accidents. A bruise had appeared near to his shoulder blade, and he kept asking me to take photographs, because he obviously couldn't see it himself. Believe me, there have been a lot of injury photographs over the years, and, I'm fairly certain, they were mostly of Hugo's bumps, scrapes, cuts, and bruises. He is athletic, throws himself around like a gymnast, and, sometimes, pays the price for it.

I still feel ill. Typical. I have a lot of work to do. When I say a lot, I mean loads. I love it! Not a moment wasted in a day, always working on a project, always thinking about the next task.

To add to my earache and cold, I received a letter from the solicitors office about V's will. Sad face.

I phoned my mum and she said it made her upset as well, plus she felt a bit sick. It's been almost a year now.

Leon had a choice of four options today, all of them education related. It's day one of another new system, another method, another way to work through the temporary school day.

Casual? Yes.

Still educational? Yes.

Less stress for everyone involved? Also yes.

Our idea to change it? Definitely. Yes. YES!

As I ranted about yesterday, we are fed up of causing Leon more and more stress.

No panic today, we hope.

No arguments today, we hope.

The professionals would probably disagree with our choices, however, other parents would probably agree. We made a judgement call. We had to.

Sawyer was angry this evening, although my notes don't say why.

Have you ever heard any of these before? If so, I hope you're okay.

I hate you sometimes!

Get out of my room!

You're fucking useless!

Can I get some bloody privacy?

I've heard worse language, and I've heard better. I'm not going to carry on with the above list, we don't need any other examples, yet I am going to take this chance to rant a bit.

Okay, context is imperative here. All the above could be used in a nonaggressive manner. I mean, if the context fit, they could be completely inoffensive, even ignored.

Age plays a part, personality as well, attitude, and, once again, the context. Let's not forget puberty as well. Wow! That always throws itself into the mix, just to exaggerate every emotion possible and confuse even more.

It sounds like I am making excuses. I am not. I am repeating the point I made in January, about seeing what is really there. When there are arguments with Sawyer, I see them differently than if they were with Leon. I see Hugo in his own way when he is angry. I do the same with other family and friends. Every situation is different.

So, back to tonight. I'm afraid to say, Sawyer *was* angry. He did mean a lot of what he said. I wish I could remember why. I wish I had put it in my notes.

In my opinion, when such words are meant, they are different from others. They're different because they hurt more. The age factor I mentioned above adds to the pain as well. As the children get older, they understand the power of such words, and that is why we find them so much more upsetting.

As you may have noticed from previous entries, Sawyer feels anger. He is nearly fourteen, so I get it. I didn't walk around smiling twenty-four hours a day at that age. I found my personality through the years.

Opinionated versus true to ones beliefs and thoughts.

Angry versus passionate, and willing to express such passion.

Stubborn versus agreeable.

Emotional versus controlled.

Impatient versus patient.

On your own versus asking for help, and being able to accept it.

I know it all versus I will continue to learn through my life.

I'm older now, I make my own decisions versus I am growing up, yet I must still respect the rules, and my parents choices or decisions.

Children are such complex little humans, aren't they? All the versus and conflicts they face during a day, and it is mostly up to us, the parents, to guide them through. It is no wonder arguments raise their ugly heads.

I know there is more on this coming in a few days, so I will stop there.

I'll balance the positive parts of the day and let the shield absorb everything else. However, sometimes, you have to go to bed with words such as those in your mind.

I do let a lot of it bounce off me. I ignore.

During the argument earlier, I told Sawyer if he ever wants to talk about why he said what he did, to let us know. We don't want him to have such thoughts, so we're here if he ever wants to talk.

We're here.

5th February.

It's the 25th of February today, and, as I was editing and typing up the notes, I just made myself laugh out loud. I also shook my head, rolled my eyes, and facepalmed.

'Town.'

That's all I had to go on.

'Town.'

I checked Mum's diary, but she wasn't volunteering, or at a parent meeting. I sometimes meet her afterwards.

Okay, so it was probably a quick run to Sainsbury's for some food?

I checked my diary. There's a receipt for an extension socket stapled to the page. Then, it all made sense.

I know yesterday was intense, and I have no desire to return to it again. However, that is how and why the argument started. I wanted to change how the plug sockets were being used in their bedroom, so a games console could be moved. Trivial nonsense.

How it ended up in a full scale argument, I am still unclear, yet I had no choice but to laugh when I saw the receipt. I apologise for my language, but really? All that drama, all that anger, all because of a fucking plug socket!

Leon studied.

'He's still feeling a bit ill.'

That line is in my notes. Maybe he rested during the day?

I worked on fixing my computer. I also researched buying a new one. It kept freezing on me, restarting, and an unbearable, random lag would slow me down. I lost a few thousand words because of it, about a month ago, and it hasn't improved since. I already thought I backed up often enough, but I had to increase it.

Mum attended a school meeting this afternoon, to discuss Leon's situation. They are helpful. More than helpful. They understand, are willing to assist in any manner permitted, and offered their continued support. No new information came from it, as far as I remember, yet it pleased us both.

Mum, Hugo, Jacob, and Leon went out later in the evening, to a parent group meeting in town. Wow! Talk about a busy day!

Sawyer spoke to me as if nothing happened yesterday. No argument, no trouble. Or, he's glossing over the surface because he knows I detest confrontation of any kind. If there is a chance of peace, quiet, and happiness, I'll take it, so I didn't mention anything either.

Right, that last paragraph probably started alarm bells ringing in a lot of your heads. I agree. They rang in mine as I edited. My silence teaches Sawyer he can get away with it? The lack of punishment or repercussions teach him there will be no consequences to his actions?

I can't comment. He knows there are rules and lines he should not cross. We know, sometimes, he chooses to cross them, and he can't yet control his emotions. What is the point of shouting, being shouted at, shouting again, being shouted at again? That's all I will say on the matter.

Over the years, I have explained how people can say words they don't mean, especially when fuelled with anger. I've shown them examples, in real life, on television, or in movies. I want all our children to realise how important it is to think carefully before they speak.

I'm proud because I taught him that, but he uses it so well against me at times!

I spent a couple of hours with Mum watching great television this evening, then checked the computer again. I think I have sorted it. Well, I wiped it and started from the beginning, with a clean system. I do hope the decision doesn't come back to annoy me.

I'm convinced I am ill as well. I have a stomach ache, plus headaches and a mild cold. I'm also convinced it is all stress related.

6th February.

Straight back to the computer this morning to move files around, and set up again. I had everything backed up, so it was a simple enough task, plus, it was a forced 'tidy up' of the computer desktop and folders. I'm all for tidy.

Remember the letter I received on the 4th? Well, the solicitors need all three of us to provide identification. (My mum and sister as well).

I thought about dropping off the paperwork to their office today. If I do, I will meet with my mum and go in with her.

Leon is still on his relaxed timetable, yet feeling ill every few hours. However, we're strict school nurses! Haha!

Get back to class, young man. You'll be fine.

He doesn't want to go to youth club this evening either, so we won't push it.

Leon slept early, so he was obviously tired.

I watched It, chapter two, with Mum. Wow! So cool. Now I have to compare it with the original. Well, no, I actually don't. I love them both. Let's leave it at that.

7th February.
Brief stint of intense work this morning. I do love to streamline my projects and tasks, or make productive decisions. If I can save myself an hour here, or another hour there, I see the difference it makes.

Time for a comedy break!

I planned everything for the solicitor visit over the last couple of days. I planned well. Now, remember those sentences. We'll need them later.

My mum calls and informs me she is about to leave. We have already arranged to meet outside the solicitors office nearest to her.

I grabbed my bag, all packed with identification letters, and telephoned for a taxi. My mum does the same.

I'm outside waiting, then I get another call telling me that my mum has left her purse and keys indoors. She never forgets her keys or purse, so it shows how much the situation has flustered her.
Also, my mum doesn't own a mobile. So, she's borrowed the taxi driver's, then phoned Mum back at the flat! Messages are being relayed to me as I travel!

"Right, I'm at the solicitors office. Heard anything else?"

"Why are you there?"

"What do you mean?"

"Your mum forgot her purse and keys. She went back home! She's waiting for you there … because you have her spare keys!"

"Oh … right. I see."

"I sent you a text. It's the taxi driver's phone number."

"Right, okay. I'll sort it."

End that phone call. Start another.

"Hi, erm, silly question, but, do you have my mum in your taxi?"

"Oh, hi. Yeah, I just dropped her outside her house. I'm nearby still. What are you going to do?"

"Can you do me a favour?"

"Sure."

"Can you go back, pick her up, then bring her to me? I'll pay when you get here."

"Sure. No worries. Hold on, I'll pull up outside and stick you on speakerphone."

"Okay."

"What's your name, mate?"

"Blake."

Some muffled noises follow, then the odd word breaks through.

"Blake's waiting … He's waiting for you …"

"Blake? Where is he? Does he know about my keys?"

"Hi, Mum. Get in the taxi. I'll pay when you get here, okay? All sorted."

"Get in?"

"Yeah. Get in. He's going to bring you to me."

"I haven't got my purse."

"I know, Mum. I'll pay. Get in."

"Right. I'll be there in a minute."

"Yeah, bye, Mum. All sorted. Cheers, mate. Thanks for your help."

"No worries."

Sigh. Sigh again.

It's not over, not yet. Remember those words from above.

"What a morning! I never forget my keys, or my purse!"

"Don't worry, Mum. We're here now. Let's get it done, then I'll take you home and let you in."

"Bloody morning!"

We hand our paperwork to the receptionist, then wait while it is scanned.

"Okay, here's all the letters back. Now, your bank details?"

Sigh.

I forgot my bank details.

I forgot my bank details?

I FORGOT MY BANK DETAILS!

I call Mum at home. Yeah, she sighs a lot as well.

Now, to add even more humour to the situation, can you answer this question? Did my mum bring her bank details?

Wait for it. Wait for it …

NO!

Why didn't my mum bring her bank details?

My mum's bank details are all in a filing cabinet. The filing cabinet is in MY FRONT ROOM!

I forgot my mum's bank details.

I forgot my mum's bank details?

I FORGOT MY MUM'S BANK DETAILS!

We sort out everything we can with the receptionist, then, while sighing so much we might pass out, go back to my mum's for tea … *and* to laugh at the absolute nonsense we put ourselves through.

"Bloody morning!"

And …

'I planned everything for the solicitor visit over the last couple of days. I planned well.'

When I arrived back home, I went straight back to work. I managed a few hours before Hugo's school run.

This morning, I asked Hugo if he could possibly come out of school today without any new injuries, bumps, bruises, stories about falling over, or similar. I even suggested a cover of bubble wrap. He had two new scrapes, so we had no choice but to laugh. I can't remember if I told him about the 'bloody morning'. He'd have called me an idiot, then joked about my memory and old age.

More work this evening. My notes don't tell me details, but it was probably a couple of hours either side of dinner. There are many short and brief parts of my business, thankfully. I can spend fifteen minutes on social media posts, or blogs. I can write for ten minutes, or edit for twenty. My time is never wasted.

Mum received a telephone call from a EWMHS counsellor, so she updated her on any and all new developments. The counsellor was interested to discuss them as well. Another review meeting was offered for Leon, and she also tried to assure us it won't be long before our help begins.

I've noticed a trait with Leon. If he has a bit of time to work through a situation, he can, and sometimes will, find a calm way to deal with it all by himself. He might overthink, but the time lets him backtrack and process. If he is surprised, told to get ready within five minutes, then face an unknown, he will definitely panic.

Will he agree to a second meeting? I'm going to place my prediction down. Yes, he will go.

I cut my hair tonight, and I think we trimmed up the children as well. They are all very different in regards to their opinion of the noisy clippers and the scissors.

"Okay! I need it cut. Spike it, and short around the sides!"

"Really? I hate having my hair done!"

"Yeah, suppose so."

"When's Nanny coming over next? She can cut my hair. You can't."

"Only scissors. No clippers."

"I look fine. I don't even need it cut."

Yeah, we've heard it all.

8th February.

All of us were chilled out here this morning. We smiled, joked, and chatted with each other.

I remarked to Mum about how much of an easier week it has been, less stressful. Yes, it's because we allowed it. We didn't push as much. We had to do it, though, we *had* to.

I really don't want to be scribbling these notes from a hospital bed, after I've collapsed from stress, do I?

My 'old friend' is back. My own anxiety. Sad face. Nervous face. Sick face.

Why? I'm blaming the week I have had. It wasn't going to put me in a great frame of mind, and I knew it. Remembering V, dealing with solicitors, and feeling as if the entire ordeal is coming to a close. It all adds up. It crept up on me.

We're also going out later, to a restaurant. Yes, I can flee from social events as well, especially if I am not in the mood to be social in the first place.

I'm hot. My heart keeps getting faster. I am trying to keep it together. It's a party. It's a chance for fun. List all the *great reasons* to go out. Yes, concentrate on the good and the great.

Nanny and May came over for their weekly visit. They made sure we all laughed while we got ready, changed our clothes for the party, then changed again, some of us a third time. Haha!

Mum said I would be fine once I left the house, and she was completely correct. I was looking forward to the evening.

We grabbed a big taxi to the restaurant, after first walking to town. We were going to travel by train, but it pulled away as we walked into the station. Typical.

Right. The restaurant was small, enclosed, and, as soon as more of the guests arrived, cramped. Amazing atmosphere, if you enjoy such a mood, claustrophobic if you do not.

Leon couldn't handle it, and he didn't need longer than a few minutes to decide that fact.

We went outside for a chat, and to try and calm down. Leon grew more and more upset, I'm afraid to say. He started blaming himself for ruining the night. It was his aunt's birthday dinner. Let's call her Sasha.

Mum and I had to call it, because a decision needed to be made. It was freezing cold, dark, and strong winds were building.

I took Leon to the nearby shop and bought him a bar of his favourite chocolate.

Internal struggles are difficult to watch, but he did stay as calm as possible. We had a lot of options to go through.

Go home?

How?

Grab a taxi from the station across the street?

Walk?

Get on the next train?

Stay and try the restaurant again?

Again, I had to call it. Leon's mind was running too fast for him to even make any sense of it.

We got in a taxi and headed home. I remember how warm it was in the car.

I made a quick cup of tea, and it also gave Leon a few minutes to fully calm down. We went over the road for some takeaway food, and I turned the television on. I didn't speak about the restaurant, kept conversation light, *and* tried to change the subject if it did come up.

About an hour later, understandably, Leon fell asleep. He is always so tired after a powerful panic attack.

I watched a few cooking shows, then, a few hours later, everyone else returned home. Nanny and Grandad gave Mum and the others a lift.

We all had a quick chat over tea, they shared stories from the past few hours, and made sure Leon was okay.

I was ready for bed ages ago, so my bed felt amazing tonight. Leon woke, then stayed up watching videos, or playing games on his mobile phone. He was calm and didn't speak about anything.

I can't say he had already accepted and moved on, because I know it isn't true. He was back in his safety zone, his home, with games and videos to escape with. Yes, a million questions were probably swirling through his mind, yet he had found calm again.

9th February.

Perfect! We all had a chilled morning, then a chilled afternoon. I can't remember which movie we put on, yet it must have been great. Haha! That sounds strange, but I haven't watched any bad movies recently, so it had to be a good one.

Mum and I looked at the debt and bills list, *again*. We often make ourselves laugh with it all, simply because we can't make any decisions, or we become confused with the thousands of calculations in our heads.

It isn't difficult. We only need to work out which ones to tackle first. The trick is NOT to jump in and pay the bill or debt with the highest amount of money owed. We find and concentrate on the ones which will save the most for us on a monthly basis.

Let me give you an example. All this is fiction, yet it should still explain the idea.

£2,000 on a credit card. £80 per month.

£300 on catalogue account A. £55 per month.

£140 on catalogue account B. £20 per month.

£300 for water rates for the year. £30 per month.

£1000 overdraft charges (You find it difficult to stay out of it every month.) £30 per month.

Okay, not an extensive list. All families are different, and have varying financial situations.

So, as I said above, it's tempting to run straight towards the credit card. Yes, you save £80 per month, but, dependant on the budget available, you could pay the others instead. You would then save £135 per month.

I believe it is always a great idea to review financial situations every six months, at a minimum. You could find a chance to save, or there could be better ways to spend the monthly wages, you know?

Sad face. There was a terrible argument with Sawyer, over something that shouldn't have happened in the first place.
Trivial.
Unnecessary.

"That's my chair. Get the fuck up!"

Yeah, unnecessary.

Again, I shouldn't have lost my temper, but I did. I justify it, though, because a bravado appeared, a 'hardman act', and I wasn't willing to surrender to it. Yes, Sawyer is the eldest, but it doesn't mean he is allowed to boss people around, or swear at them over sitting in a bloody armchair!

Horrible words, both ways. Horrible. The echoes of the 4th are still here, unresolved.

Sawyer grabbed his school uniform, so I expected him to disappear to a friend's house. I found out a short time after that it was still in his room. He'd gone outside to let off some steam. I relaxed. I definitely didn't want to be worrying about where he was for hours, then throughout the night.

After an hour, at a guess, he phoned Leon. He was on his way home, however, Storm Ciara was battering parts of the UK, so he was soaking wet. On his way, but soaking wet.

We won't speak tonight. That's another prediction. I do hope I am wrong.

My own dad left when I was only four years old. I always said I would be different. I always said I would be around, be there to teach and listen. These arguments break me. The person I am, the father I am, the father I *want* to be, when it is all thrown back at me, it really hurts. I question myself without hesitation. I *must* be doing something wrong. It *must* be my fault.

10th February.

The morning began with another argument with Sawyer. Give me a second. I need to scream inside my head.

"WILL IT EVER FUCKING END?!"

This argument was over a coat, originally, but it soon escalated. He then realised some homework was missing from his bag, and subsequently gave himself a migraine.

Bit of a backstory. He came home before Christmas with his first ever one, and it was terrifying. He didn't seem phased, or wasn't admitting to it, but we were. The sight in one of his eyes was all blurry, and all he wanted to do was sleep. Worrying times.

So, after the argument had settled and disappeared, I started to talk. I wanted to dig down, right to the base emotions. I wanted to know what was under the surface. We've tried the tactic before. It is hit and miss, but we always try.

"Why are you always so angry?"

"Why are you so upset all the time?"

"What is so wrong with your life? What has ever happened to you to make you so angry?"

We ended up talking for hours. He got stuff off his chest, however, I will keep going. I will keep digging. Some of his reasons were blatant misunderstandings. You all know by now that I enjoy a joke and a laugh. It seemed from Sawyer's answers that they weren't being taken as jokes.

Leon studied. I have to give the kid credit. In times of arguments, he will usually get as far away as possible, and finds it difficult to focus.

Mum slowly let go of yesterday's argument, and today's conversation, but it was so difficult for her.

I finished loads of work and today turned into one of my ten plus hour days.

All of V's will paperwork is done now. We shall await a phone call. My mum and sister sighed as well today, for a thousand different reasons.

Storm Ciara wrecked a lot of the local area, so the news was interesting and shocking at the same time.

Television.

Bed.

This week will see the release of the January book, so I have A LOT to complete, and many different areas of the business to visit.

11th February.

Thousands of words. Hours of work.

Leon calm and engaged in study.

Sawyer no problems before school. Can I get a high-five? Can I get a tea to celebrate?

One of the reasons Sawyer linked with his moods yesterday was a lack of privacy. I have mentioned our small home before, and our large family.

Mum changed their bedroom around a bit, tidied up, and sorted out some of the coveted privacy. He used to have his own room, but his attitude ruined it for him, and Mum needed her own space back. It was ours originally, and we had moved our bed into the lounge. Sacrifice is a two-way street, though, as is compromise.

All in all, a wonderful day, except I felt sick. Sad face. January is almost ready as well. I am on the final edits. I don't usually work in such a 'real time' manner. I mean, I'm taking daily notes, or diary entries, plus editing on a daily basis as well. It's intense, it never ends, and my focus must always be to a high level. While I am working on fiction novels, the pace can be manipulated. I can change from one project to another at will, or spend days, weeks, or even months on editing a chapter or chapters. I have worked on a few of my fiction works while writing this, and the difference is always noticed.

12th February.

Yeah, you guessed it, more edits. However, because I still felt ill, I needed lots of rest. I worked as best as I could, and drank loads of water as well. It wasn't a proper detox for the body, but it all helps.

Leon studied and branched out as well on his own English project. I do feel proud when the children write stories and use their imagination.

The solicitor firm telephoned all of us today. This week, not exactly sure when, a few more debts might disappear.

Nanny and Grandad visited this evening, but, of course, I missed it because I was in bed, resting.

Can I finish the January book by the weekend? I won't be too strict with dates. If it takes a few more days, then I won't rush it.

13th February.

Very quiet here today. Thousands of words again.

I took a short break and walked up the shops to buy Valentine's gifts for Mum. Admittedly, it wasn't a lot, but we don't waste money on one day. IT'S VALENTINE'S HERE, EVERY DAY! KISSING EMOJI. HAHA!

Another wonderful day. Smiles, laughs, and if there were any minor problems, they were dealt with quickly, so I won't even bother to mention them. I don't remember any to be honest.

We watched a movie together, yet I forgot to take any notes about which one … again. Why can't I remember any of the movies I have watched? Haha!

14th February.

HAPPY VALENTINE'S DAY! HAVE A KISS. MWAH!

Leon is unenthusiastic about his studies today. We are following school timetables and calendars, and it is the final day before half-term. As you know, we have three different schools in our lives, and Sawyer broke up from his yesterday. This, of course, is rather 'unfair' for Leon, and he kept letting us know.

We had a visit from some of the family this morning. I sold my smartwatch to Sasha, my sister-in-law. You'll remember her as the aunt from the 8th.

What to buy next?

Do I need another smartwatch?

Do I try a different style? Perhaps a hybrid?

Decisions, decisions.

Sawyer went out to meet up with his school friends today. He usually disappears during holidays, and enjoys a social life a few thousand times more impressive than ours. Smiley emoji. Winking emoji.

Leon's school emailed Mum. It was a touching note to say hello, to remind him they are still supporting him as best as they can, and they hope to see him soon.

It is amazing to know they really do care. That is exactly how I will take it.

I bought a new smartwatch! That particular decision didn't take me very long, did it?

I worked while the setup ticked along step by step. After about an hour, it was charged and ready to wear.

Jacob is obsessed with Spiderman, so I ordered a toy for him. Now, this didn't begin because of a cartoon, a movie, or anything like that. His first sight of our friendly neighbourhood crimefighter was on a console game. Hugo played it a lot last year.

Was it last year?

Anyway, the obsession started, that's the point. He saw a toy in a catalogue and asked if he could buy it!

"Me wan da."

At his age. Haha! Love it!

Mum found out she is anaemic, through the results of a recent blood test. The nurse at the surgery prescribed iron supplements.

In hindsight, Mum wondered if it was the cause for her recent lack of energy and tiredness. Busy parents take note. It isn't always the reason.

15th February.

Sleep? Hey, Sleep? Where are you, Sleep?

I've had episodes of insomnia for years now, probably since my teenage years. Okay, you're supposed to stay up late, or all night, or *even* longer when you're young. At times it's annoying, but I learnt to use it. I would write, for example, or read for hours. Perhaps my love of storytelling began with a broken night of sleep? Ooh, it sounds like an origin story. Haha! I am Superauthor!

As parenthood began, well, before in the pregnancy, my sleep patterns began to level out. I decided to try and always wake up at a certain time, always get to bed by a certain time. That used to be one of my main problems when I couldn't sleep. I would feel ready, feel tired, but, as soon as I tried, wide awake again.

It's 04:13 now. I've been awake for a couple of hours, I think. I've had a tea, flicked through YouTube, and tried to fall back to sleep. No luck, not yet.

Maybe it's because I'm excited for the first book? January will be ready for publication in a week. Well, a week is a decent estimate.

I do not set deadlines in regards to my books. I used to. Then, I discovered I was stressing myself out chasing deadlines. Yes, I stick to goals, calendars, and I manage my time, always have multiple tasks to complete, but I keep deadlines to a minimum. Instead of a set day, it will be a set week. Instead of a set week, it will be two weeks. Still organised, still strict with my workload. Less stress.

It's so quiet here during the night, inside and out. We do live near to pubs and restaurants, so it isn't always the case. We have heard our fair share of late night noise, good and bad.

At the moment, a clock is ticking in the front room, the dehumidifier hums in their bedroom, and someone is fidgeting about in their bed. Perfect time to work, some would say, even me, however, I can't concentrate with only a couple of hours sleep.

I usually end up back in bed by 05:30 - 06:00, and this morning was no different. I fell back to sleep just as the children started to wake up.

It is Saturday today and terrible weather has been predicted, so there is a possibility of us all being indoors. Storm Dennis is here, or very close, but it is definitely in the early stages.

Can we all have a wonderful beyond your wildest dreams day? I see no reason why not. Yes. Always think positive!

Nanny and May visited and there were so many laughs. Jacob was full of energy today! He ran around, jumped like Spiderman, played with May, and talked gibberish because he couldn't get the words from his head out of his mouth fast enough.

I managed to finish the edits for January, despite the company and conversations. Leon, Hugo, and Sawyer spent some time in the garden, then with Nanny and May.

Leon felt ill with a headache. He rested for a while, took some medicine, and it slowly worked.

Sawyer went out to a friend's for a sleepover, and Mum ordered a takeaway for dinner.

Jacob's toy was delivered and he played with it all afternoon. It also means we have *another* Spiderman toy in the house to keep track of. It's about the tenth, or very close to it. Haha!

The children are off school next week, so I will work tomorrow, Sunday. I can then take a guilt free day off for a trip to town for lunch, or just because I want to. If the weather isn't terrible, Nanny and May will join us all there.

16th February.

We enjoyed a quiet Sunday morning, then a quiet Sunday afternoon.

As I said yesterday, I worked on finishing January, then we watched a movie. No, I can't remember. No, I didn't take notes.

Small disagreements with Hugo and Leon. I don't know what, why, or how.

Sawyer came home. I have no notes about mood.

Do you know what? I was so focused today on January, I made very vague notes. Yeah, that makes perfect sense.

Leon worried about vegetable soup again. We tried for three hours to help him. During that time, for some relief, I deliberately made Mum laugh. We both needed it.

How?

By acting out pornstar poses on the bed, of course. Yes, I remained fully clothed.

Calm returned for the later part of the evening. I expect we managed a couple of hours of television.

Made Mum laugh again. I think it was a joke about gnomes or elves. It's a private joke. It's aimed at me. I don't mind and join in all the time.

The will money appeared in my bank just before I went to bed. Mum was already asleep, so I showed Leon and Hugo. I also took a screenshot because it will be different in twelve hours.

17th February.

I phoned my mum as early as possible today. We had a quick chat about the money. She is all for treating the children, and has planned to do so for about a week now.

I transferred money to Mum's account, as we had agreed months ago. She will juggle the numbers around, then pay some bills later today.

Work today? Of course, but what to do? Something book related?

It is only nine o'clock. I've drunk half a cup of tea and I'm on finances with Mum! Haha!

We moved money.

We spent money.

We looked at how much money we had spent.

We looked at the bills, *and* how much we will save.

We both told ourselves how our hard work, patience, and saving had finally brought us to a better place, financially. Let's not forget, as you may recall from the January introduction, this all began in 2018.

Okay, I had a few moments of weakness, I admit. I thought about walking to town and buying a new laptop. I told myself to behave and act responsibly. I probably (definitely) growled at myself.

Hugo, Jacob, and Leon watched a film. No, don't even ask. I have no idea! Haha!

I worked and released January. Now I can concentrate on how to market it for a couple of days. However, I also can't stop. I must continue with the daily notes, the edits for February, and preparing for the second book.

Kept making Mum laugh a lot today, by asking her for a refund. Haha!

"Yeah, I've changed my mind. I want my money back. Forget the bills, I want an iPhone 11!"

It didn't work. Winky and laughing emojis.

I played a fun game with Hugo, a football quiz. He loves everything football. The game made us both laugh, a lot. It was great.

I built a chair this evening, and wasted at least forty-five minutes on one screw! One screw! I know. Riddikulus!

I watched television with Mum, after we both finished growling at the chair.

Everyone here seems happy, and that gives me another reason to smile.

18th February.
Today started with a planned visit to town. I told the children about Nanny's generosity and, of course, they needed to go out to the shops. There was suddenly money to spend!

Mum and I wanted to go to the bank anyway, to deposit money used yesterday for a few online purchases. Yeah, there will be a lot of indecision and returning to certain shops multiple times. Hey, that's shopping with children, though, right?

Hugo doesn't even know what he wants, but there are a few ideas moving around in his head.

I was correct. We were in town for three hours ... ish. In and out of different shops. One of them always grabs our attention. It's a kind of tech, gift, toy, I-don't-quite-know-what-it-is-or-why-I-want-it-but-it-looks-so-cool shop. Even Mum and I love it.

Hugo bought everything! Haha! Okay, no, he really didn't, but he had a bloody good try.

I grabbed a couple of interesting items for the office. One was an awesome desk fan that has a clock on the blades, in LED lights, and the other was a magnet ... Erm ... It's a magnet base with loads of metal balls on top. You can move them, or make cool designs. Okay, I'm not selling it, am I?

We arrived home after lunch. I always tell the children, usually a minute or so before we reach the front door, how they're going to help us unpack before anything else. I bet you can imagine how it works out? I also don't want boxes and packaging all over their bedroom floor. The bin and recycling bag are ten to twenty steps away. Not far to walk, I assure you!

I checked all their receipts and change to make sure it all added up. It did, just about.

Mum noticed a sudden toothache. She was fortunate with a short notice appointment and booked herself in for tomorrow morning.

Hugo and Leon disappeared to their bedroom, played, and talked about all their new stuff.

This is a bit random, but I bought loads of plants last year. It all began after V's death. Unusual side effect, I agree, and I can't explain it. Anyway, Leon got his first today, an echeveria, so we spent some time together repotting it. He is interested in gardening, I think. He acts interested, let's put it that way.

After my stint of financial mastery, I caught up on the notes for this book. I should really learn how to stop. No, I know how, I simply choose to work instead, if possible.

It's half-term now for the children, so they have time off school. It is also easier for us to chill. We're all less ruled by the clock, by school drop off and pick up times.

I created an instagram post about January's book. I also have random days from this project on a blog, so I have other parts to keep updated.

Sawyer was home late, and by late I actually mean later than we ever want him out in the evening.

I told him in an earlier text message that we need to get it sorted. We sit here worrying, and he can't spare two minutes for a message?

Wow! I am so glad this teenage phase is here. I also wish there was a font for sarcasm.

Television.

Bed.

However, it was a restless night for Mum, unfortunately. Apart from the toothache, she was also aching all over. The cold is horrible here at the moment. Chilled to the bone is quite an old-fashioned term, yet it rings true with the current weather and storms.

19th February.

Mum went out early to her dentist appointment. It's an infection, so she was prescribed antibiotics. I had to joke about the amount of tablets she is taking at the moment.

We went back to town to buy a few specific items. I am so glad we live close by. My leg muscles are also glad, believe me!

A bulb for a lamp was one of our must buys. Leon is very particular about his sleeping habits, and we are also particular about which lights are turned off at night. The lamp is a compromise, plus getting lost on the way to the toilet is almost nonexistent now. Haha! I actually laughed while typing that sentence!

There were a couple of slight issues with an expected parcel delivery, and the children not being able to sign for it. I don't mean they weren't allowed to sign by the delivery company, they just didn't want to. Yes, you read it correctly. They didn't want to.

It makes me laugh when they are so awkward and shy. They can scream and shout at me, or Mum, or each other, but they can't answer a door.

Yeah, like I said, it makes me laugh. Do they not realise we can see through the bravado? It's a parent superpower. True story.

While out, I also wanted to, once and for all, get the Wi-fi in this place working properly. We have upgraded in the past. It didn't work. We bought an extender plug. It didn't work either. Well, it was a bit temperamental. Yes, our Wi-fi might not be the fastest, and it might be temperamental as well. Plus, there are so many devices trying to use it now. There weren't five phones ten years ago, there wasn't a Netflix subscription, there weren't games consoles and online gaming with friends two miles away.

Today, I bought a mesh system! Yeah. I really did. So far, it's solved the problem straight away. £70.

Why didn't I do this sooner? I probably didn't have a spare £70, that's why. Or, when I first looked, it cost double or triple the amount.

Hugo helped me set it all up, and I gave the new Wi-fi a stupid name. Well, it made me laugh.

I worked on some side tasks during the afternoon. I want to place some book orders, so I have some stock, and I want the best prices for those orders. I also formatted for a new book, not one related to this. What else? Networking, and, of course, a bit more writing.

Sawyer and Leon decided they would bike into town and buy some clothes.

They didn't try the clothes on.

The clothes didn't fit.

They didn't keep the receipt.

Sigh.

Guess what I did earlier? After we returned from our visit to town? Yeah, that's right, I put all the important receipts away.

Guess what the diaries from the last three years look like in my office? Yeah, that's right, they have receipts stapled inside of them. So many receipts.

One day, legend tells us all, children *will* listen.

We all spent a chilled evening together, however, we had to sit Jacob in the 'naughty corner' for a couple of minutes. He is starting to be a bit too rough with his brothers during play. We want it stopped before it goes any further, for him to understand it isn't acceptable, and we will do our best to teach him.

I'm tired. I need sleep. Jacob napped today, so he might not sleep until nine, or later. We shall see. I also refer you back to the 15th. I might be tired, but I'll be up until at least eleven o'clock, minimum.

Yawn!

20th February.
Straight to work this morning. No, wait. Straight to work, *after* tea.

Sawyer is out with friends again, Mum and Jacob are in town for a meeting, and Hugo and Leon are here with me. They're playing, eating all the food, or taking it easy.

I researched a few marketing ideas, and there are many to choose from. Some decisions will be based on price, some on personal preference, and some because I've never tried them before.

Change of plan for the afternoon. I am off to the games console maze for a couple of hours. Leon's friend won a competition, so we paid for him to join in. He asked if one of us would stay, though, and I volunteered. I will use the time for these notes, edits, or social media work. Never a second wasted, although, I may pick up a controller for five minutes. I mean, honestly, I'm rubbish unless I get into a game, so I'll get laughed at if I do play.

After dinner, I had a relaxing bath, then a chat with Leon. We didn't talk about anything specific, and I used the time for encouragement.

Quiet evening with television. Definitely a great day.

21st February.

I had another broken night of sleep. There's nothing in my notes about why it happened. I do have a tendency to wake up and make a tea anyway, simply because I know it's going to happen.

It feels like a 'slow' day this morning. Time ticks by, minute by minute.

Sawyer is out for a bike ride. However, he took Leon with him, then disappeared to meet with his school friends further past the town centre. Leon called me because I think it panicked him a bit, being alone all of a sudden. It shouldn't have, because he does bike around on his own, but not usually to the town centre area.

I didn't leave here to meet him, as he wanted me to, but I talked him through the walk home.

Leon and Hugo are both in, playing games consoles. I'm working, as per usual. I need a holiday! Haha! I know, once all this hard work pays off, I'll treat everyone to a break. Deal?

I planned some marketing again today, and set up social media accounts for the new book. I also checked order prices for the upcoming paperback, and edited February.

After dinner, we walked up to the shops for chocolate and alcohol. Haha! What a wonderful combination. I'm glad Mum is going to have a couple of drinks with me and let herself relax for a couple of hours.

It wasn't long before the music channels went on the television! We sang, danced, and laughed. The children told us to stop singing, dancing, and laughing.

"Dad," said Leon.

"Yeah, mate?"

"You either sound pretty good, or terrible."

"Okay. Erm. Okay!"

We crashed out somewhere close to midnight. Hugo and Leon wanted to play on the console in the front room, so they kept asking me why I wasn't in bed yet, and hinting that I should go to sleep. My own children told me it was time I went to bed! Haha!

22nd February.

I woke up later than usual this morning. I blame the lager!

Halfway through the morning, I chatted to a counsellor friend at a local shop. He is the one involved, but not involved, with Leon. It was only a brief conversation and update. He isn't sure which direction the therapy will take, however, we do agree on the end goal.

It is a Saturday, so Nanny and May visited. Chat, as usual. Laughs, as usual. Feeling a bit tired, not so usual. I blame the lager ... again.

Sawyer finally bought the school shoes! Fireworks! A round of applause! A cheering crowd! Oh, sarcasm, how I love you.

In the spur of the moment, I decided to go to town, and I took Jacob with me for some company. I have no problem whatsoever acting childish when I am out with him. I sing, laugh, talk in silly voices to him. Yeah, I get a few stares in the street and shops, but it makes me smile, plus I don't care. Haha!

I bought two pairs of jeans, and a plug socket for the office. It has USB ports. I can feel the jealousy. Haha! It should help with my bundle of wires. No, wait, I am already a tidy person. I have a set space for my desk, and everything on it, underneath it, or in front of it. It's about a metre square, so it has to be used well.

I felt so tired again once I returned home, and it stayed with me through and after dinner. It's only six o'clock and I could so easily go to bed!

I reminded two of the children, Sawyer and Leon, that they need to get ready for school in a couple of days. Uniform, bags, and everything else. It was a carbon copy from the 5th of January.

I know Leon hasn't got to think about school as much, but he must be in the correct mindset. He must realise that Monday morning means back to study.

I received an email today, linked with marketing for these books. I'm excited and ready for next week.

I gave Leon and Hugo a small 'reminder' about tidy beds, but I think I went to bed annoyed. That is never a great idea, not in my opinion.

23rd February.
Half argument. Heated discussion? Explain?

Erm … I would, if I knew what I was talking about. No more notes to go on, so I can't elaborate.

Not good enough! Do better, Blake! What is the point of notes if they aren't useful?

Sawyer and Leon went out on their bikes. Leon called me about an hour after, and I joked with Mum about not answering. That sounds a little harsh, but it was meant in jest. He has always been told to check in with us, or let us know if he is going somewhere different than originally planned.

Okay, an update. He crashed on his bike. Nothing too serious, but the frame hit him, and it hit him hard.

This is a great example of Leon's mind running towards the negative.

"No friggin' hospital! I'm not going to friggin' hospital!" growled Leon as soon as he came home.

As you may remember from early January, Sawyer went in for surgery on his leg. Leon has told himself he *will* need to go through it as well.

We spent ten minutes calming him down before we were even allowed to have a look. He took some ibuprofen, then rested on a bed.

In our opinion, it wasn't serious. It definitely wasn't as serious as he believed. He will need to rest, there will be a massive bruise, MASSIVE, and it will hurt for a while.

Mum needed to stock up on certain foods, so we went to town. We should move even closer, shouldn't we? Anyway, she isn't on a diet, although she used to be, but she still eats healthily.

Leon felt better, so he went back out on the bike. We made it clear he is to be careful, phone us if he needs to, and come home if the pain returns.

For some unknown reason, and this actually happens quite often, I have a sudden upset, down feeling. Meh! Isn't that what everyone says? Meh! I don't know. I just feel … down. It will pass.

The afternoon ticked along while Hugo played on his console and watched YouTube. Jacob and Mum sat in the front room, cartoons on, laughing at his superpower.

Our neighbours dropped by for a quick cup of tea. We chatted and their kids played with our kids. I also sorted out my new smartwatch with their help, because I needed to link it with an Android phone.

Within half an hour, four thousand toys had made there way to my front room. No exaggeration. Okay, maybe a little bit. Three thousand.

Dinner, then a relaxing bath and shave. Jacob kept saying he needed one. Haha!

"Me, Daddy. Me need yave too!"

'Yave.' Brilliant!

Television with Mum to end the evening.

Quick chat with Hugo before bed. Again, he couldn't sleep, so I provided the company.

24th February.

I woke up early today to the beautiful sounds of a newly set, birdsong alarm. Don't wake up to loud noise from alarms, that's my advice. It can be very detrimental to your mood.

Hang on a minute. Didn't I put this in the introduction? A part about parents waking their children up? I think I need to copy and paste.

Alarm clock. A gentle and polite alarm clock. Children want to be woken up as if a cute kitten has crawled in the bed with them, purring with a gentle rhythm.
"Come on! It's seven o'clock! Up, breakfast, get dressed!"
How dare we? Such cruel and unusual parents.

Erm … let's change the subject. Okay, okay, we'll have a quick chat about the contradiction I have just discovered.

I promise you that by the time we say 'Come on! It's seven o'clock! Up, breakfast, get dressed!', we have already tried five to ten times. We have already purred with a gentle rhythm.

Sawyer off to school.
'He had a verbal dig at Leon before he left.'

That line is in my notes. I expect it was to do with the first day back at school, because Leon did try the unfair angle again. Mum and I stopped it in its tracks. He isn't going to swear or talk to us with anger.

Loads of work, and Leon studied as well. I placed a few book orders, and researched marketing again.

Mum and Hugo went to the cinema. Yeah! What a lovely treat and break away for them both. He isn't back in school until tomorrow, and it gave us a chance to reiterate our thoughts, the ones I've mentioned before about always finding some time for him.

I tried to solve a marketing issue, or obstacle. I won't upgrade it to a problem, not yet. There must be a way, I simply haven't found it yet.

The Outsider by Stephen King. Have you watched it? So good! I have not read the book, yet.

So, apart from a glitch here, a few words there, today was wonderful.

25th February.

I had some time alone to work this morning. Mum and Jacob took Hugo to school, accompanied by Leon.

Nothing unusual in those sentences, I agree. However, Leon planned to walk his school route. Yes. He is pushing himself and trying. Proud face.

As if by magic, it is a couple of hours later in the day. He did well! No panic! I'll let out a huge sigh of relief, a cheer, a high-five, let off some fireworks, drink tea, have a biscuit, kiss Mum, hug Leon. You get the idea.

Guess what happened during my work this morning? I finally solved my marketing issue. Awesome!

Leon studied, and there were no problems. Sometimes, a push, a battle with the anxiety, it can linger. I hope he is proud as well.

Jacob, as usual, was so funny today. He will be three in the summer, yet his humour is so strong already. Sometimes, he gets the timing just right as well. Okay, that part is probably coincidence, or is it? Haha! He came and told me Mum was playing on the Xbox. She wasn't, but it gave us all some laughs.

After a school holiday, I feel different. Not alone. I have never been bothered by being on my own. It's just the flat feels empty when the children are not here. I'm so sentimental at times. Don't tell anyone. Shhh! Winky face.

I think I will take a break from edits on the computer over the next day or so, rest my eyes a bit. However, I do need to update Instagram and push the marketing. Maybe later, after dinner? I can also print off the notes and work the old-fashioned way, with a pen and paper.

Mum is laughing at my singing. Haha! The children the other night, now Mum as well? I'm actually joking. I know I won't win any singing contests, although if I want to, I can rock it!

Do you remember I told you how Hugo loses his temper when a certain word or term is used? It must have been in the January book? Well, Leon has one as well, but, it is a nasty word. I have been trying to stop it for a while now.

I was in the kitchen with Mum, then I heard an argument in the front room between Hugo and Leon. A push, a shove, 'Get off me!', that sort of thing. By the time I had walked three steps, it was all over, so I left it and spoke to them after dinner.

I spent twenty minutes with Sawyer and Mum sniffing oil burner scents. Some were amazing, some were strange, and some were … not so amazing.

Sawyer wrote 'NO!' on all the ones he considered gross or disgusting.

I finished with work at six, so a long day today. Well, I moved to the sofa to post about work on social media. Haha!

26th February.
Mum went out with Jacob early this morning, straight after Hugo's school drop off. It was another meeting for her voluntary parent work.

Leon and I ran an errand for about an hour. It involved a lot of walking, so we always class such activities as physical education. Got to stick to the school timetable!

Hours of work for the rest of the morning for both me and Leon. I also decided to meet Mum and Jacob, and combine it with a quick shopping trip. I wanted to pick something up for Jacob.

Just as I was getting ready to leave, the attendance liaison from Leon's school dropped by for an update. We had a brief conversation, and made sure we are all still on the same page. It is encouraging to speak with, and see, these people. Sometimes, because they are detached, they notice changes in behaviour, mood, or state of mind. Comments were made on how Leon seemed more relaxed.

Mum laughed at me in the shop! Haha! We walked through the gardening section, and I saw some gnomes. Yes, as you know from the 17th, gnomes are part of a private joke here. I also saw bags of inexpensive and great quality soil and compost. Okay, I may have shown a little too much excitement. Excitement about … mud. What can I say? I enjoy gardening.

I worked for the rest of the afternoon on marketing and other books.

Nanny and Grandad visited this evening. Laughs? Yes, of course. He refuses to grow up as well, so we get on like a pair of jokers.

We told Leon and Hugo to try and go to sleep a little earlier this evening. They do stay up too late talking, then it's difficult to get them out of bed in the morning. Haha! My copy and paste from two days ago rings true once again!

So, another day full of wonderful. What is that now? Three in a row? I mean, if a day here has gnomes included, it means we're laughing, so it has to be FANTASTIC!

27th February.
Work. Work. Work. Oh, and don't forget work.

My publisher and I have arranged for some great marketing on the January book. Can't wait! It starts tomorrow morning.

Cheeky Jacob scammed extra biscuits out of us this morning! I'll say it again. Cheeky! It wasn't a complicated plan. He asked me, I said yes. Then, he asked Mum. She also said yes. Scammed by a two year old. We need to up our game.

I have a slight headache, but I'll push on. I probably need to move away from the computer screen for an hour or so.

I nearly got blown away when I took Hugo and Leon to their youth club. Wow! The weather here is intense at the moment. I have to admit, it makes me laugh when I get pushed around by gales. Hugo finds it funny as well.

We watched a series about local crime tonight. Some of the locations shown were literally around the corner!

I want to start watching more of those shows, and crime documentaries as well. Maybe I'll write one? I do love a good mystery.

28th February.

Straight to my computer, well, my mobile phone, however, the marketing doesn't start for a couple of hours. I don't want to say it, but I can be impatient at times. I know, shocking, right?

Quick town visit, then to work for the rest of the day. Mum, Jacob, and Leon went out to an afternoon meeting.

Nearly at the end of month. Wow! Another month gone by already. I might not even bother with meeting management. They'll want to dissect my every thought. We will see.

Other marketing ideas, so I'm going to research those, and, more importantly, their costs.

Our evening was chilled, yet overshadowed by Sawyer not coming home from school. Let me explain. He is reluctant to text, phone, reply to texts, answer phone calls, especially if they're from us. You know the deal. We're spying on them. We're controlling. We need to stay out of their business. We need to give them privacy. He's very close to turning fourteen, so I do get it. Independence kicks in, the sense of freedom, the ideas of making his own decisions and choices.

Anyway, ten o'clock at night. That's when he finally came home. We knew he was with friends, indoors in one of their houses, but that was the only information we had.

Do you remember this from the 18th?

Sawyer was home late, and by late I actually mean later than we ever want him out in the evening.

I told him in an earlier text message that we need to get it sorted. We sit here worrying, and he can't spare two minutes for a message?

Wow! I am so glad this teenage phase is here. I also wish there was a font for sarcasm.

We decided not to say anything when he got home. No, we're saving that lovely task for the morning.
Sad face.
'Do I have to?' face.
'This will be fun, but I am actually being sarcastic' face.

I overheard a chat in their bedroom, one he started with Leon. *Something* happened after school. Kids were shouting at each other, I think, or there was an argument? Parents turned up to shout as well and help their kids?

We'll find out, eventually.

But, but, but …

Why do we have to? Why weren't we told earlier? Why aren't we being called with explanations? Why are we sitting around until ten o'clock, completely oblivious to the situation?

Yes, there are a million more questions. Probably several million.

29th February.

Ooh, a special day. To all of you with a 29th of February birthday, have a wonderful and amazing time!

I'm slightly jealous, to be honest. It's a cool 'thing' to have in your life.

I was up in the night again. Two o'clock? Tea, then back in at four? Maybe five? I can't remember.

Sawyer started to explain, with a dose of added attitude, after we asked a few questions. I wasn't bothered about the why. No, I was, of course I was. I also needed him to know how worried we were, and how unacceptable it was to walk through the front door without any calls or texts.

His attitude grew worse because he knew a long and possibly angry chat was about to start. Plus, let's not forget, it doesn't take a lot to light his short fuse. We'll blame him. We won't understand.

Yeah, we might, and we might not. However, it's a two way street. If he never talks to us in the first place, if he makes it difficult to even talk to him, our frustration will only grow with every deflected or avoided answer.

As last night for Sawyer involved others, I will not list the details. Yes, there was an incident. Yes, it got out of hand when it shouldn't have.

Like I said, I'm less bothered about the why.

Mum and I had to endure Sawyer's anger and bravado throughout the explanation. As predicted, we got it all. I'll copy and paste, *again*.

You know the deal. We're spying on them. We're controlling. We need to stay out of their business. We need to give them privacy.

Mum and I remained calm. I didn't want to start my day off with an argument.

I was on the phone to my mum during much of his loud rant. Her thumb was painful during the night, so she might not be over to visit today. We could go to her house, so we'll decide on that later in the morning.

A calm covered everything, suddenly as well. I don't think any of us could be bothered to continue. I'm not sure which direction to go in now. Our chat on the 10th proved Sawyer does need to talk more, open up, so maybe I'll revisit when I feel the time is right.

Hugo went to a birthday party for a couple of hours this afternoon. He was also sick in the car on the way home. Yuck! Too much running around, jumping, excitement, plus he isn't great with car travel.

My marketing looks good. I'm confident it will achieve its purpose. Okay, that sounds corporate and straight out of a manager's handbook. I'm excited. I have a goal and this will reach it. Yeah, that's much more casual.

I haven't had a chance to research any other possible marketing choices, not yet. I think I will post a paid advert. You know, like the ones you see on Instagram or Facebook?

Hold on …

Sorted. I think. I'll add in a curious emoji. If it is approved, it will run in the next week.

No Nanny and May, however, I still had to phone her about four times. I wanted to check on her and the pain in her thumb. Also, we're trying to sort out a washing machine recall. We tend to make the telephone calls on her behalf, then update her with any news. It's easier.

The argument with Sawyer this morning is hanging over us. I don't want another later, or tomorrow. He will either be home and make a massive deal out of it, or ignore us. My money is on … erm … coming home on time. Yeah. I'll commit to it. I'll believe.

I took a brief walk with Mum, Jacob, and Leon. It's always a good idea to grab some fresh air and stretch out the legs, even if it is only for half an hour.

March tomorrow! I wonder if I should speak with the management team?

No, unfortunately, I was wrong. Sawyer came home later than we asked, and complained to Mum on text messages beforehand. We hadn't made it clear, we never said he *had* to be in, only to be told where he was ... and other such nonsense. There isn't an emoji for my emotions right now, so I can't put one in.

"Hi, Blake."

"Erm ... Hi. Sorry, who is this?"

"My name is Constance Miller. I'm part of the management team."

"Oh, right, yeah. By the way, great name!"

"Yes, well, thank you."

"So, how can I help?"

"Blake. This conversation has been arranged for over a month now. I've left messages, emails, reminders. Surely you've received them?"

"..."

"Blake? Are you still there?"

"Yes. Yes, I'm here."

"Are you ready?"

"I am, however ..."

"However?"

"Do you have the notes there, from my chat with ... erm ... Michael Page? From the end of January?"

"Yes, I do. They're a little ... vague. We can add to it now."

"Oh. Okay. That kind of backfired on me."

"How do you feel about the past month, Blake?"

"Well, I ... erm ... yeah. Good and bad. You know? Loads of laughs. Loads! We've worked a lot on our happiness. We know we need to bring it back to the home, so we're doing it."

"I see. Bringing happiness back to the home."

"Are you making notes?"

"Yes, Blake. It's all for the monthly report."

"…"

"Some of your decisions were very successful. Some were … not so much."

"Well … I'm no expert. However, I do everything I can. *We* do everything *we* can."

"I see as much, Blake. The only criticism I have is that you try and remain calm. I know you can do it. *You* know you can do it."

"Thank you, Constance."

"Also, follow your instincts. If you believe it to be a good idea, or you disagree with someone, say so. Instincts are part of the job. Judgement calls and decisions made in less than half a second. You will make thousands more, so believe in them, and don't cover yourself in guilt if it doesn't *always* work."

"Yeah, I see your point."

"Great, Blake. So, we're done. I enjoyed it. See you at the end of March."

"Okay. Speak soon."

"Oh, can you do me a favour?"

"Yeah, I'll try, Constance. What do you need?"

"Remember to write down the titles of the movies you watch?"

"Right, yeah. I'll try."

Chapter three

March

1st March.

It's a Sunday. So far, it's also been quiet.

We had one of our usual visits from Mum's family, and it took up most of the morning. It's a great way to break the drag you can sometimes feel on a Sunday.

Sawyer and Leon went out together. For some reason, they biked all the way to visit the family they'd seen earlier! It made no sense, but they told us it was an unplanned trip, and Sawyer also needed to borrow a phone charger for ten minutes.

I rearranged my office after buying a new piece of furniture. Blame Jacob for his influence.

What am I even talking about?

Okay, have you ever heard of a trunk novel? It's a term known in the book world. It can mean an unpublished book, an unpublished, *terrible* book, or unfinished manuscripts that the author will revisit one day.

I have trunk novels. I also have a lot of notebooks and folders containing my current works. I say current, yet I am only human. Haha! I can only work on so many at a time, and others will be put away.

Guess what? I don't own a trunk. Sad face. However, Jacob owns a large wooden toy box, one that is also a double seat. Yeah. You can see where this is going now, can't you?

There was a stint of heated discussion at dinner. I don't know how it began, but it was linked to us all moving house this year. I remember I said ridiculous words because of pure frustration.

"Do you know what? New decision! You lot behave, then we'll move. Okay? Not the other way round."

I don't know where it came from, or why I bothered. I know I am not serious, but I think I was at the time.

How much can I take? I do not know the answer. I do know … I do know I am struggling, and I am miserable as soon as an argument begins.

VEGETABLE SOUP! VEGETABLE SOUP!

Go and check the 3rd of February. Leon had vegetable soup! Amazing!

We are so happy. We are! This is a giant step forward for him. Seriously, we'd throw a party if we could.

Had a shoot out, Spiderman web-slinger style, with Jacob. Haha!

He won.

2nd March.

Right, let's do this!

New week.

New month.

Positive vibes and outlook.

The sun is even shining this morning. After the weather we have had for months now, I need it so much. I do enjoy the warmth from the sun. I wonder if I should get one of those 'SAD' lamps? Do you know about those? Research

'Seasonal affective disorder'. There is information on the NHS website, or just Google the terms.

I arrived home after Hugo's school drop off, made a tea, then went straight to work on marketing and advertising. My budget is minimal, so I had to target the adds specifically. Parents, mums, dads, and as many associated to them as possible. I'll cross my fingers. It can be a success, a failure, or, the numbers look great but nothing comes from it. So, it seems to be successful, yet it isn't. Yeah, that makes sense, I think?

Leon is studying, and still smiling about his vegetable soup. He asked about a reward for the achievement yesterday. If I'm honest, and Mum agreed with me, we thought it would have been a super pizza. Near us, there is a takeaway restaurant that sells an eighteen inch monster! He's had a few before, and one of them was definitely linked to a school reward as well. Instead, he asked for a half day off 'school'. So, in reality, he wants a break from his studies. I agreed without hesitation. It's such a win.

I wonder if I will eventually explain all the codes I've used later in the year? Perhaps I will put a list in at the end of the final book?

Anyway, back to work! After I make another tea, of course. By the way, my office space is less cluttered. I love it. My new double seat, it's-not-a-toybox-because-I'm-too-old-to-call-it-that, my place to store my many notebooks, also smells of freshly cut pine wood! Awesome!

Jacob is being so funny at the moment. For the past couple of weeks, he's been trying out different voices. He goes deep toned, then high, talks while feigning laughter, or mispronounces words because he knows it will make us all smile. Brilliant!

He literally did it two minutes ago, so I had to add it in here. More of the wonderful beyond your wildest dreams, as promised, right?

Mum showed me an interesting post on social media earlier. It's about a small group nearby, for homeschooling. We have emailed the people in charge, *and* they are eager to meet Leon. Watch this space.

Time for tea. Shall I ask someone here to make it for me? I might get lucky.

So, we're going to check out the new school group later in the week. It removes a hurdle straight away because it is based in a familiar location, and very close to home as well.

Leon's usual school want to set up another meeting. There is always need for more discussion in regards to the next step in the process. We all want to move forward with the medical tuition.

Jacob painted some brilliant pictures today. His pride and joy was a snowman. We tried to put it on the wall, but it upset him because he wanted to hold it. Haha!

My notes say we had a calm evening. FANTASTIC!

3rd March.

I was up in the night for a couple of hours again. Tea and YouTube for me. Why is it happening so much lately?

We are not sure if the tumble dryer is protesting, or losing the will to carry on with its job. Maybe retirement? I have no idea how old a tumble dryer has to be before it leaves work and collects its pension.

Right, marketing. Come on! Sell some books!

I managed a couple of hours, then went for a quick visit to town. I needed to pick up a new vacuum cleaner for my mum.

Update on the tumble dryer! UPDATE! This news just in. It caught FIRE! Shocked face!

I was with Leon, carrying a large box on my shoulder. We were ten to fifteen minutes away from home, then the phone rings. I can't answer it, because of the box, so Leon does it for me.

"Dad, Mum is panicking. She needs to speak to you. I don't know what's wrong, or what she's going on about!"

"Okay, mate."

I put the box down as I start to run a few million scenarios through my head. Don't you love imagination sometimes? Yeah, sarcasm detected.

"What's wrong. Are you two okay?" I asked.

"... Out the back door ... on fire ... grabbed the tumble dryer ... okay ... shaken up ... fucking hell!"

"What the fuck?! You're both okay, right? We'll be home in ten minutes. Drink a sweet tea."

"Yeah ... yeah! We're okay. Jacob didn't even realise! He's watching cartoons!"

"Don't panic. We'll be home really soon."

She's tough, but Mum was shaken, understandably. She said her mind was running at a million miles a second, deciding on when, or if, she would need to call the fire brigade.

Worked on these notes and edits for the rest of the day, and made a point of checking on Mum every few milliseconds.

There are only four weeks today until the end of March. Four weeks will move fast. That seems to be another side effect of these books, as I mentioned earlier. Time is blurring once again.

Leon studied during the afternoon. He's still smiling because of his vegetable soup! So are we!

After dinner, we had to try out the launderette around the corner. Our new tumble dryer doesn't arrive until the weekend, and we have a few loads of washing to finish.

It's exciting for a geek like me. Apparently, the new tumble dryer even has an app! What? Don't laugh.

Leon had vegetable soup again. It means it is over, well, part of it is over. Erm … how to explain, *and* stay in code?

Okay, there is a larger, or related issue, and vegetable soup is part of it. The other issue still needs addressing. Yeah, it wasn't that difficult to explain.

Sawyer was in a calm mood this evening. It's great to see. Now, let me explain. It's nothing to do with the peace and quiet, or the fact there are no arguments. For us, we want him to feel happiness. We want him to be in great moods all the time! He shouldn't have such an angry weight on his shoulders at his age. He turns fourteen in under two weeks, not forty!

4th March.

Mum went out to a parent meeting. It's very important, and I'm so proud. MEGA-SUPER-PROUD! She is a speaker for some new parents joining the voluntary programme.

I might go to my mum's and drop off her vacuum cleaner, plus, there's a kettle here as well for her. It is easier for us to pick up items from town. The travel is too much sometimes. We can walk in and back within forty-five minutes, and our legs are a lot younger than hers!

I went to my mum's and tried the new vacuum cleaner. It was a great opportunity to give her house a spring clean, so I did. I have been talking to her and Mum for a couple of weeks now, about helping more.

Picked Hugo up from school, and we started to discuss floating in a swimming pool. Haha!

"I can't float."

"Of course you can. Everyone can. It is one of the scariest parts of learning to swim, but it is true."

"Nah, I can't. I must be different from everyone else."

"Yeah, okay. You can float, trust me."

Sawyer was frustrated at dinner. Not certain why, but he started talking about Leon being absent from school. I have a theory, so I will share it with you all.

Back in January, I told you all a story. I asked you to imagine you were a parent having a bad day. By the time you reached dinner, you were angry, frustrated, and impatient.

We're guilty of this. Sawyer has linked some of these instances with Leon being at home from school. If we have trouble with Leon during the day, we're angry by the end of it. If we subsequently argue with him, or ask him to tidy his room with 'a bit of attitude' in our voices, that is why.

Email accounts and passwords. I have so many. I should streamline, yet I'm a bit too busy for side tasks at the moment. Maybe soon. It would make life a lot easier.

We were both very tired tonight, but we had to watch the end of a television series. We had to see how it ended!

(Constance, I promise I am not trying to annoy you.)

5th March.

I have had enough of this terrible weather. I think *everyone* has had enough of this terrible weather.

Okay, I live in the UK, near the coast. I should be used to it by now. Moan, moan, moan. Right, that's out of my system.

Worked for the entire morning on marketing. Afterwards, I wished I had a larger budget for marketing.

My mum wants to put a memoriam piece in the paper for V on Monday. She's not pleased with the price. The last time we did this was back in the early nineties, for my uncle, V's husband, so it is more expensive now.

I'll write it out and add all the names for the family. I have sixty-five words to use, so that will be plenty.

Leon wasn't too excited after his visit to the homeschool group, the one I mentioned on the 2nd. If anything, it made him upset because he realised there is no option but to push himself. He doesn't know how, so it scares him to think about the future. Of course, we will continue to talk with him, reassure, and give him some time to process.

My afternoon was focused on writing and edits. I left the marketing research and tasks for today.

I got soaked on the school run for Hugo! Have I mentioned the weather? Yeah, I know I have!

Sawyer complained about the planned dinner. I spoke to him, calmly, because I am worried about a different issue, much more far reaching. I mean, I am often worried about his anger, and the attitude which shadows it. I'll try to explain.

He is not learning any of this behaviour from me, or us. No, wait. This is difficult to contextualise.

Yes, he has seen me lose my temper before. He has seen Mum lose hers as well. However, he has also seen us control ours.

I DO NOT complain to Mum if I have a problem, or don't agree with something. EVER.

It's a bit of a family meme, but we often laugh and tell people we have only ever had three arguments in our entire relationship. It's true! We never raise our voices with each other. We never argue. EVER.

But. It's a big but, so I need to put it in bold and capitalise. **BUT**, it only takes one person to think I am influencing Sawyer, that he is learning from me. I can't even imagine having such a thought associated with me. It's the complete opposite of my core values in life, my moral code, call it whatever you will.

Thankfully, a quiet evening followed. Mum felt a bit sick, but she was okay. It caused a restless night, but nothing else, thankfully.

6th March.
Mum still felt ill this morning. We'll keep an eye on it. I know she has been eating some different foods, and trying out a few recipes in the past couple of weeks.

Now, Jacob loves to copy us. Our words, our actions. He also copies from the television. I work at home, usually on a computer, and I know he has seen people using computers while he watches television as well. For example, his beloved Spiderman, or Ironman, tap away on keyboards. So, he began to sit down, quite often during the past few days, and type on an imaginary one.

"Hey, Jacob. What are you doing?"

"Me on my dom-dooder."

"Oh, you're on your computer?"

"Yeah."

"Okay, well, you have fun. I'm going back to work. I'll be at my desk."

"Oh-day. Me go bah-do-wer."

"Yeah, you go back to work."

Absolutely brilliant! Haha!

Due to this imaginary awesomeness, we decided to buy him a learning laptop. ABC, 123, a is for apple, e is for elephant. I love it! Jacob loves it!

I can't believe it's Friday already. Another week of words, of tapping away on my dom-dooder! Haha!

I noticed today, again, that Hugo is in the background. He can't be there, as I have made perfectly clear before. We'll make sure he knows that we know. If he knows that we know, then he won't worry, hopefully, that we don't know. You know? Confused face emoji. Haha!

Leon and Sawyer took a couple of bike rides before and after dinner. They don't go far, well, not all the time. A quick ride around the block, a bit of fresh air, an hour out of the house.

I wonder what tonight will bring? Movie? One I will forget the name of? (Sorry, Constance.) Television?

Jacob is jumping around in front of me as I type this entry into my phone. Love it!

7th March.

I went into town with Jacob for a walk and some fresh air. 'Lovely day.', scribbled in my notes. I expect the sun was shining, and the cold winds finally disappeared.

Nanny and May over for their Saturday laughs and chat.

I messed around on my computer, trying to design some watch faces. No idea if it will work. If it does, I can create my own for the new smartwatch. Cool! Okay, my geek is showing again, I know.

Sawyer and Leon went out on their bikes for a couple of hours.

I decided to give myself a refreshing haircut. My usual style is clipped around the sides and back, very high, then a grade 6-8 on top. Smart and easy to manage.

No arguments. We all seem to be smiling as well.

Late to bed tonight. I had to get in touch with my friend, the Tooth Fairy, on behalf of Hugo. She's very real, as we all know. Of course, she is!

This prompted me to search for a clip from Peter Pan. It is one of my favourite scenes.

I do! I do! I do believe in fairies! I do! I do! I do believe in fairies!

I then went on Google to see if Wendy was the same actress from the recent BBC adaption of Dracula. The amazing and sarcastic, humorous, you-don't-scare-me-vampire, Van Helsing.
She wasn't, but for a moment I wasn't certain. There is a similarity.

Hang on, did I have a proper day off work today? What? That never happens!

As you can see, today was quiet and WONDERFUL.

8th March.

Remember Sawyer's school shoes? I wrote about them on the 22nd of February, although I am sure I mentioned it before that date. Anyway, they weren't any good. After one day of use, they were deemed rubbish. I don't know why I didn't rant about it before today.

I want it sorted. I want it sorted once and for all. Sawyer is wearing shoes with split soles, and has been for a couple of weeks!

Some of Mum's family visited this morning, so more laughs and chats. Weekends are quite a social time for us, and it is a welcomed break from the Monday to Friday rush.

We needed to pick up a few presents for Sawyer's birthday, so, yet again, we went to town. Jacob and Hugo were with us today. Leon went out to meet a friend, and Sawyer did the same.

Did he take money with him for school shoes?

No.

Okay, I know we never see Hugo, and I know I have mentioned the family meme quite a few times. However, he must 'save up' all the news, all the conversations, and ALL THE WORDS in his head.

Why?

Because he talks, constantly. He tells us football stories from school. He tells us football stories from his console. He tells us other stories from school. He tells us other stories of no relevance at all! Random questions, random tales from inside his brilliant, and very humorous, mind.

I even made a point of telling him.

"You know what, mate?"

"What?"

"You can do this at home. You can talk to us there as well. You don't have to store it all and blurt it out in one hour."

"Yeah, I know. I'm too busy at home."

"Busy? Playing football games?"

"Yeah, and watching Youtube."

Leon decided to meet us in town because his friend went home earlier than expected. He walked in and joined up with us all at one of the shops. However, there was an immediate misunderstanding over how much money he had to spend.

"Nothing," said Mum.

"What do you mean, nothing?"

"I checked your bank account the other day. It's empty. You've spent all your money. Christmas, your birthday? You spent it."

"No. That's not right. I had some in there. The last time I asked you, it was twenty quid, or close to it."

"You must have spent it. Try and remember what you bought recently."

Leon disappeared inside his own head, turned on the calculator, plus the memory files. He stayed there for ten to fifteen minutes, then returned.

"Nah, something is wrong. I didn't spend any money. I didn't. Okay?"

Our patience began to wear thin. I told Leon to retrace all his recent trips to town.

"You topped up your phone. I remember that."

"Right, Dad, but I had … twelve quid left over."

"What about stuff in your room? You've bought a few bits."

Then, the penny dropped. Leon remembered where the money had gone.

"Damn it!"

He sulked for a minute or two, then carried on with his day, accepting of the mistake.

Sawyer was out. Sawyer was in. Sawyer was back out. No shoes yet. Sigh.

9th March.

This is going to be an interesting week. We will have a fourteen year old soon. Fourteen! Shocked emoji!

I felt ill today, so did Leon. He went back to bed this morning.

Hugo and Sawyer went off to school without any noted issues, and Mum and Jacob attended a parent meeting.

I worked, as per usual, but I needed to keep taking breaks. If I have to, I will go to bed early.

I don't usually take days off ill. I don't get ill very often, touch wood. Yes, I really touched wood when I wrote out the sentence! My new, and very cool, pine seat. Oh, yes!

I've suddenly remembered I have to check something. I hope I am not too late, because it has to be finished and ordered by a certain date. Back soon!

Update. All done. Took me a while, because I needed to make sure it sounded correct. I placed V's memoriam in the local paper.

We finished watching The Outsider on television. Aaaarrgghh! Amazing!

Leon's stomach hit him harder than mine. He appeared to be in a much worse state than I was. Due to this, we had a late night.

10th March.

The painful stomach aches are still lingering, unfortunately. Yes, Leon's still feels horrible for him, and he still has bouts of pain.

Loads of work, despite not feeling well. To be honest, I'm glad for the distraction. The marketing and social media posts are ticking along in the background, so I can concentrate on edits and new work.

I had a few laughs with Hugo on the way home, yet no notes on why. No doubt it was because of a ranted story about school, or football.

I took it easy for the early evening, in the hope it relieved some of my symptoms.

We are going to start a new television series later this evening. I've wanted to watch it for ages, so I'm excited. Mr. Mercedes! I blame Stephen King, and The Outsider. They are linked due to one of the characters.

Side note. All I hear about at the moment is the coronavirus. I'm not worrying, not yet, although it has struck nearby, if the news is to be believed. Apparently, local supermarkets have been cleared of certain items as well. The panic buying has already begun. Sometimes, it's difficult to keep the worries away.

I'm sorry for today and yesterday, I truly am. I feel as if I haven't been at my best because of those random stomach aches.

Oh, before I go and rest, I want to add some school news regarding Leon. Mum received an email today, from the attendance team at his school. They mentioned that emails sent to the counselling team haven't been answered yet. I would be disappointed, and that is the most polite term I can use, if Leon's help is being hindered by email issues. I mentioned research for private counsellors, and their costs. If we can afford it, should we?

I just had Mum in hysterical laughter! I do love an innuendo. I usually don't care how rude they are, especially with Mum, and say them wherever and whenever. I deliberately held my lips shut, so she burst out laughing! Haha!

11th March.

Yuck! I feel worse today. I went back through the manuscript and found the entries on the 12th of February? Cramps, nausea, and tiredness. I know I have to be careful with certain foods, so maybe I ate something I shouldn't have?

I missed a few hours of sleep during the night, again. I wonder if there is something on my mind? That can be a cause. It has been in the past. Sometimes, I don't realise it's there. I don't realise what is on my mind straight away.

Leon returned to his studies for the morning. I went to town, only a quick visit, and was in front of the computer by ten. Today is reserved for edits. Serious, get it right, check-it-and-read-it-a-few-times-before-you-move-to-the-next-part, edits.

We have lovely weather here today. Oh, I love the sunshine! I can smell spring in the air!

By the evening, I felt better. Once again, I raised my water intake. In my opinion, I should do it more.

Have you ever tried it? Have you put yourself on any sort of detox? I don't go too far, but I feel the difference with even a few glasses of water added in during the day.

Nanny visited tonight, but no Grandad. He is out with people from work … *again*. Mum's brother and his girlfriend came over as well.

I joked with Nanny about Grandad's social life. He never used to go anywhere, however, there have been more work dinners arranged recently.

Leon and Jacob fell over on the way home from Hugo's school. When I say they fell, it was only Leon, but he was carrying Jacob. I will put this here, so it is in print and recorded forever. WE WERE SO VERY PROUD of Leon's reaction. He hurt himself because he instinctively moved his body to keep Jacob safe.

I know, it was amazing to witness. I explained it to him, the reason why we were so proud. I also told him he had passed a 'Dad' test. Haha!

Mum received another email from the attendance department at Leon's school. There had been an issue with the email systems. Don't worry, I won't type out hundreds of rude or offensive words. I'll just sigh.

12th March.

Mum and Jacob went out for a parent meeting and crèche, if it's available. If not, the children play together in the same room.

Leon studied, and I worked on more marketing options.

We had an unexpected, 'cup of tea length', visit from Mum's uncle. He wanted to drop a card in for Sawyer's birthday.

I feel much better, however, rather unfortunately, today was the day when a lot of politicians held press conferences about the coronavirus pandemic. I had BBC news on in the background, so I caught some of the details. It is bordering on terrifying. Okay, it might sound like an exaggeration on my part, but when I look at the numbers, that's how I see it. Now that governments are admitting it is spreading at such a rate, worldwide, our concern has grown.

I finished February. Cheering crowd? Well, maybe. I haven't stepped back and let others read it yet. For all I know, it could need another few edits, or be a pile of horse shit.

Do you remember I wrote previously about deadlines? Well, not so much a deadline, but I like to keep a maximum of two weeks between these notes and their edits. It seems to be a workable system. I'm ahead of myself by one day at this very moment. Awesome!

We worked through quite a busy few hours after school. There was Hugo's pick up, a visit to the shops for extra Sawyer presents, drop off at youth club, home for a quick dinner, pick up from youth club, then, finally, home again.

We mentioned to Leon that he will be stepping up his studies a notch next week. We want a few 'push himself' situations included. There will be rewards, so he is willing to try, even though, to him, some are giant steps. To him, some are as serious as vegetable soup.

13th March.

Happy birthday! Happy birthday, Sawyer!
He's fourteen. Fourteen! Of course, we haven't aged a bit. Winky face.

He liked the presents and money we gave him, even though there wasn't an extravagant mix. He ate a few of his chocolates before even leaving for school. Haha!

We have a birthday takeaway for dinner planned, however, do you remember my story from the 4th of January? Well, Sawyer wants to eat from *that* specific fast-food restaurant. I have already decided I will go to town, buy it, then get home as quickly as possible. No delivery. NO!

Jacob is hilarious on birthdays. First of all, it's his birthday.

"My bir-day."

"It's Sawyer's birthday."

"No, Daddy. My bir-day!"

He also wants to open all the presents. He takes ages to get through wrapping paper if he does get a chance to help with any.

What else? He hassles me to make Alexa sing happy birthday. I started it last year, so it's a family meme now. I think we asked her about ten times before Sawyer even made his way to the front room. Haha!

"Bir-day cay?"

"Yes, you can have some birthday cake later."

Brilliant!

There was a slight panicked episode from Leon this morning. I got him through it with distraction, and *no other choice*. I didn't take notes, but I do remember it was in regards to leaving the house.

I tried to figure out how to name the books. To be honest, with hindsight, it would have been easier if I hadn't split January as its own Kindle book. Now I have to work out a separate set of titles. Good one, Blake, very clever. Facepalm.

I now have five Kindle books planned, but only four paperbacks, and I already have the titles for those paperbacks. Right, hold on, let's see if I can work this out here and now.

Erm …

No. I paid attention to my mathematics teachers, and it doesn't add up. There will be a way to sort it. It will no doubt involve some random idea, or different titles for the paperbacks. Yeah, it could be as simple as changing titles, couldn't it?

We have planned to go out tomorrow morning, and it was somewhat of an impromptu decision. Due to the coronavirus fears, the shelves in shops and supermarkets are becoming bare. Mum and I want to try and grab a few essentials, just in case, you know?

14th March.

We managed to grab everything needed while in town. Yes, there were empty shelves, but still plenty of stock. I suppose timing is an issue as well? If a shopper arrives two minutes after new stock is put on the shelves, it won't seem as bad as they've heard.

Nanny and May came over for their usual visit, slightly overshadowed by the escalating news. Jacob fell asleep on the way home from the shopping trip, but woke up to see them.

I tried to design a watchface today. It didn't work, not the way I was doing it. Still, just a bit of fun. *However*, it will grate on me until I solve the reason. Haha!

Mum is keeping herself well informed about the coronavirus news. We heard about a friend of hers today, one who has put herself in self isolation. Shocked face.

Decisions will need to be made. The children might need to be kept off school, and very soon. I'm worried parents will avoid the playground as of Monday morning.

This sounds ridiculous, but I want a tent, although Mum says no, it's unnecessary.

Hey, my idea is focused on isolation. So, isolate in a tent. I mean, I will be outside the window in the garden. I won't be far away.

I can't believe how strange this is, *and* how rapidly it has become so. I'm talking about my idea, and decision, at the end of last December to write about a year in my life. It is now looking as if it will cover the coronavirus pandemic. A diary of the progression. Utter madness.

Sawyer went out with friends, birthday related, so I was told.

I need a tea! I thought I'd share that with you all. Haha!

Hugo and I spent an hour or so solving a Rubik's cube together. He was obsessed with them for quite a few months, either last year or the year before. This one is not easy, because it isn't of the normal design. Google 'windmill Rubik cube'. We have spent hours together trying to solve these, and we have some of the patterns and algorithms down to memory.

We ended up calling it at about seven-thirty. The video tutorial we were referring to cut out, and it annoyed us both. Haha! I rage quit on a Rubik cube!

Jacob is currently fist-bumping me, plus all his toys are as well.

In regards to yesterday's title dilemma. How about an extra untitled book about parenting? Yeah, that fits. Then I can continue with the other planned titles, and there will only be one 'extra'. I can make it clear on Kindle and paperback formats. Plus, let's be honest, the months are printed on the cover.

15th March.

As soon as we woke up, rather sadly, we checked the latest coronavirus news. I already know a lot more will feature in these books.

We have spoken about this together, as a couple, as a family, and as parents. Some of our thoughts are based on news, some are based on foresight. The next few weeks … months … maybe a year, are uncertain. It sounds like such a leap, such a horrific prediction, yet the scientific numbers show it to be true.

I want to speak to my mum today about being careful. I want her to stay indoors as much as possible. Mum's the same with her parents. Wish us luck. Wish us all the luck. Parents who work, who socialise, who enjoy walking to the shops, driving to the supermarkets, they will not take such advice with open arms.

Jacob wants me to go back to work with him already! It's only eight o'clock! Haha! Okay, I sometimes start earlier during the week, but it's a Sunday. He's a strict boss!

I went into town for school shoes with Jacob. Yeah, I still hadn't sorted Sawyer's, and I needed new ones for Hugo as well. It wasn't a panic buying, apocalyptic, or crowded scene as I had feared. I could hear people discussing it, though, and quite a lot of them.

Home for a relaxing bath and shave. I'm trying, *trying*, to fill my mind with other thoughts, other than those revolving around the coronavirus. It's taken over the news, though, and that proves I should be thinking about it.

I played with Jacob, although I have no notes on which game or activity. Trust me, it would have been full of laughter.

All in all, we enjoyed a chilled day with nothing but normal, the good kind of normal, and wonderful. I only wish I wasn't so scared of the news.

16th March.

I woke up at 'about' two o'clock in the morning. I probably would have gone straight back to bed, but I read a story on the coronavirus and it made me overthink. It made me overthink *everything*. I can't remember when I got back to bed, but a cup of tea would have been involved along the way.

Sawyer is off school today because of a stomach ache and nausea. He is a voracious reader of the news, so I hope he doesn't see anything that worries him too much. Or, it's already happened?

We have workmen due over today, so I moved to the front room. Jacob joined me, of course.

"Bah-do-wer, Daddy?"

"Yes, back to work."

Too cute.

There's a show on children's television, and Jacob giggles every single time he sees this crab character. He falls on his head and Jacob sits there laughing.

I had to go into town for a few office supplies, then try and find the food that was missing off our delivery. Yes, panic buying and stock levels are linked at the moment.

When I arrived home, the workmen were nearly finished.

So, how are we are going to have the *serious* conversations with family members? They must happen, yet I can't answer my own question.

Today was the first of a new schedule, daily, for government press conferences. We will be given updates, advice, expert analysis, and scientific data. The tone from the beginning was one of resolve, and the need for change. The entire country was, for want of a better word, told, to change their daily lives. Told to change their habits and routines.

Change. Change, because more will die. WILL DIE. If we don't change, the numbers will be horrific.

The advice from the government directly impacts quite a few of our family members. They are classed in vulnerable groups.

17th March.
We all went out on Hugo's school run, plus a short errand afterwards.

Leon was going to try his old school route this morning, but he wanted to go home and study instead. He was talking with Sawyer last night, so I can see where the brief urge came from.

Sawyer is off ill again, and he won't be in school tomorrow because of a staff shortage.

After a couple of hours of work, it is obvious to me that everyone and everything is now about the coronavirus, and on a worldwide scale. I am interested. I want to know how the world is dealing, and how we will recover, in all areas.

I don't want this to evolve or change towards a coronavirus diary, no, but I will include any and all I see as interesting, or relevant. However, I may not be able to stop it from happening. Yes, this is a parenting diary, a daily peak into our lives. It's all linked. It's all woven together in the family.

I mean, for example, I have already thought about staying at my mum's for a few days. I might buy a cheap phone as well, so we can video call her. She is in a vulnerable group, so she should stay indoors and protect herself.

Actually, I haven't mentioned certain information in these diary entries yet. Information about May.

You may have noticed already that when I speak of May, it is always alongside my mum, and there is a very important reason for that. May has mental and physical health issues, and those issues have been present from a very young age. She cannot be without my mum, or another member of the family. She is not classed in the vulnerable groups, yet you can imagine why we have to include her in our worries and future plans.

Mum's parents are both in vulnerable groups as well. They are in work, so there are other factors to consider. They have bills to pay, they don't want to be fired from their jobs if they do decide to self isolate, and they need money to be able to buy food.

The end of the month approaches and, despite all the news and fear, I can't wait! Excited emoji! I'll know how the marketing worked for the January book. Plus, because this second part of the series will also be complete, the first paperback can be released. Awesome!

I have to say, it seems chilled out here, relaxed, although I think we're distracted into a stunned disbelief with the news, and all that follows on from it. I know the children, excluding Jacob because of his age, are thinking about it as well. I wonder how their minds are processing such a crisis? I wonder if we are projecting a calmness towards them?

18th March.
The shelves were rather empty in the shops today, and a lot of people have been posting about panic buying on social media.

It is regularly mentioned on the news as well. We managed to buy most of what we needed, although it is obvious that certain items are being considered more essential. Paracetamol, well, basic medication of all kinds, hand sanitiser, nappies, toilet rolls, and bread and pasta. This isn't an exhaustive list by any means, but you can see how the mindset is unfolding here in the UK.

I put the BBC news channel on all day today, and it was dominated by coronavirus updates.

One of our friends has gone into self isolation. She has a fiancé, and two sons. As far as I know, it isn't a confirmed case, and she is only following the government advice, yet it is terrifying to think this virus is literally on our doorstep.

I worked mostly on these notes for the day, but the news was my main priority. Some marketing was thrown in, plus some editing as well.

After the press conference today, school closures have been announced, as of Friday afternoon. As a parent, we knew it was coming. It has already happened in other countries, so it was only a matter of time.

How will this decision thread through our daily lives? I can't answer.

How will Leon take it, knowing he hasn't got to think about going back, for the foreseeable future? I can't answer.

Will Hugo see another day of year 5? Again, I'm sorry to say, I can't answer.

On the subject of Leon, he took another giant step forward today! Awesome! It sent him into a panic, but he did it. I treated all the children to pizza as a reward.

Nanny and Grandad are over for a visit. I wonder if we can get them to understand my thoughts on all this?

My mum will probably be here on Saturday, with May, so I will have to arrange something with her. However, what should I do? Weekly visits? Staying over? Shopping for her? She won't leave the house, not unless it is an absolute necessity.

I know, I sound like a government spokesperson, but I see a bleak future, very bleak, unless we all listen to the advice.

I was about to go to sleep, but I had an urge to type out all my thoughts. This week has moved in rapid, unbelievable moments, and I think I, along with many others here, are having trouble keeping the pace. We need to take regular moments to catch up, then, something else happens and we start again.

The school closures, for an indefinite amount of time at the moment, is a perfect example. Those responsible for children, all over the country, have a couple of days to find interesting and innovative ways to find educational, productive, and creative ideas.

Everything is changing. Much has *already* changed.

Think about it for a moment. Children might not see a classroom again until September, possibly even further along in the year. This will include the summer holidays and months of warmer weather. During that time, new changes or advice from the government could alter life again … and again … and again.

I am shocked, pensive, scared, and many other words I won't type here. If I did, this book could end up with a gargantuan word count.

I have never been involved in anything like this before. I don't think there is a person in the world with experience of such a global fear. Such a sudden global change and upheaval. The world has changed in a couple of weeks for us, longer for others. If you go back a few pages, you will see the entry on the 10th of March.

'Side note. All I hear about at the moment is the coronavirus. I'm not worrying, not yet, although it has struck nearby, if the news is to be believed.'

Eight days. Look at how much the world has changed in just eight days.

Our personal emotions change by the hour, sometimes by the minute. We worry how the children are processing it all.

How do they really feel?

Do they understand the situation properly?

Do they feel the same weight of concern? Is it possible for them to? I hope not, I really do.

To me, the pure coincidence of these books during this time is nothing short of unbelievable. In a way, I am glad I have the opportunity to record a diary for our life at this time.

In the space of a week, my entire mindset, my focus has shifted, evolved, morphed. Some is under my control, some is beyond it. We have no choice, though. We have to accept this, *have to*, and adapt our lifestyles and behaviours to fit these new social rules.

I think my thoughts have calmed, now it's all down as notes. I should be able to sleep.

19th March.

There are already new routines. We wake up and *immediately* check the news. We wake up and *immediately* worry about how much the world changed overnight.

I am going to watch the news all day while I work. I want to hear everything. Although it is terrifying to hear some of the developments, there is also a strong desire to soak in the knowledge.

Sawyer is in school today. Hugo is at home because his closed a couple of days early for an intensive cleaning operation. Leon is, as you know, not in school at the moment anyway. We have been trying to gauge his mood, and his feelings on what is happening.

The government has set out plans for the children of 'key workers' to stay in the school environment. These people are needed to be in work.

We aren't going to be strict teachers, and that decision wasn't difficult to make, if I'm honest. This isn't the normal way of life, in any sense, so why do it? There is already plenty of educational material online, and on the hundreds of television channels as well. That is also the government advice, so we will follow it. Schools have also recommended websites.

Today, in a news sense, was what I will call a scientific day. There was lots of information about the virus, statistics, data, why it is spreading, how to go forward. It is interesting to learn how the scientific community is attacking such an unknown and major challenge.

Nanny and Grandad, Sasha, and my brother-in-law should really be off work, because they are classed as vulnerable, named in the 'at risk' groups, but we haven't heard anything from their employers yet.

In the terms of these books, the original terms at least, it was a quiet day. The wonderful beyond your wildest dreams has a dark cloud over it now.

HOWEVER …

We see wonderful elsewhere. All the good spirit, care, and nature being displayed throughout the world.

Even the government are impressing me, and I do not say those words without weeks of thought. I *need* a lot of convincing when it comes to showing my respect.

The children are convinced they won't see school again for months, possibly not until the next academic year. I don't know how to answer any of their questions.

20th March.

I know the government isn't running on a Monday to Friday schedule, yet today is the end of the first 'press conference' week. I'm unsure how the weekends will be addressed.

It's been the week of change, the week of turning the country on its head, of creating a new way of life. Call it what you want. I don't think anyone in the UK will ever forget it. I even joked with Hugo yesterday on that very topic. He'll tell his children about it one day, after they've studied it in a history lesson.

"I was nine when the virus hit."

"You were there, Dad?"

"Yeah. My school closed. I couldn't see my friends. Nanny and Grandad were scared, but we all got through it."

"Wow!"

Shops. I can't remember if I went alone, or with Mum and the children. I know I stared at empty shelves with a sense of worry.

I think I will begin formatting on the paperback today. How exciting is that? Well, I'm going to take any chance to smile at the moment.

I worked for the morning on edits, although I was focused on the news as well. I am one week behind the notes, so, going by the loose-ish deadline rule, I am ahead of myself.

I developed a sudden headache, so I stepped away from the computer for an hour.

Leon and Hugo seem to be adjusting to the school closures, although it is only the first couple of days. Of course, we expect a very different attitude in a couple of weeks, or a month. Sawyer is off school now as well. He told us there were about twelve children in for his year today. All three of them have been sent work to keep them occupied, so we will add to it as well.

Tonight, at the government press conference, the Prime Minister, Boris Johnson, closed all cafés, restaurants, bars, clubs, and entertainment venues.

I see such a different world around me. This entire year will be unbelievable.

However, life goes on. I expect we will walk around the shops tomorrow, all of us or just a couple, and pick up the essential items we can find on the shelves. I believe the panic buying will slow down. I sincerely hope it does.

Again, the government impressed me today. The chancellor of the exchequer, Rishi Sunak, set out incredible financial steps for the year. His aim, in line with Boris', is to protect the people of the country. I have to say, I am glad for the press conferences. They have become a part of my day, and, let's not forget, only since Monday. It proves how important I regard them.

I hope to see Nanny and May tomorrow, but I will have to check again in the morning. Any signs of illness, even unrelated to the Coronavirus, and we will have to say no. I had already planned to go to her house next week, to help with some housework and gardening. Unfortunately, all decisions are day by day for now.

On a completely different topic, one of the marketing steps I used for January ends next weekend. I don't think I will set up another, not straight away. I will check the results, good or bad, then decide. If it works, *if*, quite a few parents will read the January book in the following weeks.

Want to know a secret? I always get nervous at such thoughts. Is there an emoji for that?

Daddy stinks! Whatever. Haha!

For no reason at all, Jacob got off the armchair, then came over and sniffed me!

I don't stink! I promise!

Haha! Brilliant!

21st March.

Come on! It's seven o'clock! Up, breakfast, get dressed!

How dare I? Such a cruel and unusual boss ... to myself. (That all sounds strangely familiar. Winky face.)

Sawyer stayed at home, yet the rest of us went to town to try and get some more essential items, and the children have a bit of money to spend as well. As I've said before, it's so much easier to get them out of the house if they have cash. Haha!

So, the essential items. Bread, pasta, rice, milk, headache tablets, specifically paracetamol, dinners for a few days. We managed to buy most of it, and it was much quieter than usual everywhere in town. Jacob is too young to understand, but Hugo and Leon noticed the difference. One of the shops had stopped taking cash payments, due to infection risks. It is a surreal world.

We didn't hang around. In and out, nothing unnecessary. We were on a mission, you know?

Nanny and May came over, but only after I spoke to my mum about everything. We all washed our hands, kept our distance, and there wasn't any physical contact. We decided, regrettably, that we will discuss limiting any visits to a couple of weeks, or more. Decisions are difficult to make, because the world changes, new rules and restrictions are set, or medical advice arrives, and it arrives hourly sometimes.

The children are smiling today, so I have to claim wonderful beyond your wildest dreams.

Here's a thought. I wonder if I will class every forthcoming day in the same way? I mean, as long as everyone in my life remains healthy, what other way can I see them?

It's four o'clock now. The press conference centred on shops today, due to the panic buying, but the Prime Minister wasn't present. Personally, I hope he took a short break, and remember, these people have to earn my respect. I don't give it away without good reason.

I would like to help more, and volunteering seems to be an option. I have a website to visit, so I will let you know of any developments.

I might have to visit town again tomorrow, for a new microwave oven. Ours is protesting as much as the tumble dryer did, and we all know how that ended. If I do, I'll look for essentials again. Every chance we have to pick up items in the shops, we must take it.

There are loads of stories on the news showing humanity at its finest. I love them. I LOVE THEM! It isn't a percentage of good stories against bad, it's more like rays of sunshine through a dark cloud.

Sawyer and Leon are off out on a bike ride. I have told them not to be too long, and to adhere to the social distancing measures. I made sure they heard my words.

It is Mother's day tomorrow. I haven't bought a lot, but I will make sure they both feel special.

22nd March.

As I have already mentioned, decisions sometimes need to be made. So, it was the last family visit for a while today. We all know it is the correct way to move forward, even though we don't want to. We have vulnerable people through the joint families, plus the children, so we will never regret it.

I sent some messages out on social media to friends, close by and around the world. It was a simple hi, hello, hope you are well. Many of us are being told to stay indoors now, as much as possible, so social media is going to be vital for the world.

I went out to town for two main reasons. One, I wanted to buy a new microwave, as I briefly mentioned yesterday. We don't need any appliances breaking on us at the moment. Two, I have almost decided, for certain, that I am going to live at my mum's for a week. She wants to stay in, to listen to the government advice, so the company will be positive for her and May. Any food needs can be arranged by my other sister, I think I named her Jasmine, or Mum. Even the children could bike over to her house and drop off a loaf of bread, or a bottle of milk.

It wasn't manic in the shops, yet the store assistant I spoke to said the morning had been.

P.S. No microwaves in stock.

I'm waiting for the press conference. I have also started to pack a bag. I don't need a lot as I'm only planning on a few days. I will pick up some food on the way tomorrow. I will also walk there, I expect, instead of using a taxi. It's such a torn decision, one with negatives regardless of the final choice. I don't want my mum and May alone for three months, possibly, and I don't want to be away from Mum and the family either.

The children were slightly frustrated today, but they went into the garden to get some exercise and fresh air. I understand, I do, but they have to as well. We're in this situation now, together. There is no choice.

Of course, I could go to my mum's in a week, or two, or a month. You will know when I know.

23rd March.

Monday morning. It feels like … every other day in the week. Haha! Do you lose track of days when the normal school holidays are on? I definitely do.

Mum tried the shops this morning. Not much luck with many items, unfortunately. She will go back later and try again.

Okay, here's what I have decided, after overthinking and sleeping on it. I am going to go to my mum's today, after I try the shops for her. There are a few supermarkets near her house, so I'm optimistic. I'll follow all the hand cleaning rules, be as safe as possible when I am inside her house, and there will be no physical contact. I'll then decide if I am staying overnight, or coming back home.

The shops were empty. Both of food and of people! There is an eerie vibe on the streets. I did, however, manage to get most of my mum's list, so that is great news.

I spent a few hours with my mum and May, ate lunch, chatted, and tried to reassure her that she won't be alone in the following weeks and months. She knows it to be true as well, but it doesn't stop the feelings of encroaching loneliness.

I bought a couple of packets of noodles on the way back home. They will make someone a quick lunch. Leon loves noodles.

Mum was fine here with the children, and they spent time in the garden again.

The press conference for this afternoon has been postponed because of a COBR meeting. For those of you that don't know details about UK politics, COBR is an acronym for Cabinet Office Briefing Rooms. They are offices in London used for urgent meetings.

Of course, we naturally wondered why. As far as we're all being told, and by all I mean the British public, there will be an important announcement later this evening. The Prime Minister is to address the nation, or a very similar event. It may turn out to be less formal.

Hugo had his hair trimmed while I was out. Nothing major, only a clipper grade around the edges and back. Mum dyed her hair a purple colour today as well. I suggested we all do it. If not now, when this is all over. The children were not convinced, however, and Sawyer and Hugo have had highlights before! I thought they would go for it! Haha!

Time for a tea. I have a couple of hours before the announcement, so I will update afterwards. Everyone, or at least the majority of the country, believe we are about to begin an enforced lockdown. Yeah, it's happened elsewhere, and now it is serious enough to do it here.

I actually joked with Leon the other day. I reminded him of how I asked for a different year. It had to change. It's all there in the introduction, and subsequent days of January. I did not have any idea how it would actually happen. I think the super-busy, tea-spilling Universe went out, got drunk, then collapsed all over the office!

On a work note, I edited some of the publishing channels today, and I may add other books as well in the morning. Apparently, it will help in overseas markets, so that will be amazing.

Right, tea. I'm not putting it off any longer!

I can copy and paste from the government website. It states it is a transcript of the speech, so I'll trust that information.

Good Evening,
The coronavirus is the biggest threat this country has faced for decades —
and this country is not alone.

All over the world we are seeing the devastating impact of this invisible killer.

And so tonight I want to update you on the latest steps we are taking to fight the disease and what you can do to help.

And I want to begin by reminding you why the UK has been taking the approach that we have.

Without a huge national effort to halt the growth of this virus, there will come a moment when no health service in the world could possibly cope; because there won't be enough ventilators, enough intensive care beds, enough doctors and nurses.

And as we have seen elsewhere, in other countries that also have fantastic health care systems, that is the moment of real danger.

To put it simply, if too many people become seriously unwell at one time, the NHS will be unable to handle it - meaning more people are likely to die, not just from Coronavirus but from other illnesses as well.

So it's vital to slow the spread of the disease.

Because that is the way we reduce the number of people needing hospital treatment at any one time, so we can protect the NHS's ability to cope - and save more lives.

And that's why we have been asking people to stay at home during this pandemic.

And though huge numbers are complying - and I thank you all - the time has now come for us all to do more.

From this evening I must give the British people a very simple instruction - you must stay at home.

Because the critical thing we must do is stop the disease spreading between households.

That is why people will only be allowed to leave their home for the following very limited purposes:

- *shopping for basic necessities, as infrequently as possible*
- *one form of exercise a day - for example a run, walk, or cycle - alone or with members of your household;*
- *any medical need, to provide care or to help a vulnerable person; and*
- *travelling to and from work, but only where this is absolutely necessary and cannot be done from home.*

That's all - these are the only reasons you should leave your home.

You should not be meeting friends. If your friends ask you to meet, you should say No.

You should not be meeting family members who do not live in your home. You should not be going shopping except for essentials like food and medicine - and you should do this as little as you can. And use food delivery services where you can.

If you don't follow the rules the police will have the powers to enforce them, including through fines and dispersing gatherings.

To ensure compliance with the Government's instruction to stay at home, we will immediately:

- *close all shops selling non-essential goods, including clothing and electronic stores and other premises including libraries, playgrounds and outdoor gyms, and places of worship;*
- *we will stop all gatherings of more than two people in public – excluding people you live with;*
- *and we'll stop all social events , including weddings, baptisms and other ceremonies, but excluding funerals.*

Parks will remain open for exercise but gatherings will be dispersed. No Prime Minister wants to enact measures like this.

I know the damage that this disruption is doing and will do to people's lives, to their businesses and to their jobs.

And that's why we have produced a huge and unprecedented programme of support both for workers and for business.

And I can assure you that we will keep these restrictions under constant review. We will look again in three weeks, and relax them if the evidence shows we are able to.

But at present there are just no easy options. The way ahead is hard, and it is still true that many lives will sadly be lost.

And yet it is also true that there is a clear way through.

Day by day we are strengthening our amazing NHS with 7500 former clinicians now coming back to the service.

With the time you buy - by simply staying at home - we are increasing our stocks of equipment.

We are accelerating our search for treatments.

We are pioneering work on a vaccine.

And we are buying millions of testing kits that will enable us to turn the tide on this invisible killer.

I want to thank everyone who is working flat out to beat the virus.
Everyone from the supermarket staff to the transport workers to the carers
to the nurses and doctors on the frontline.
But in this fight we can be in no doubt that each and every one of us is
directly enlisted.
Each and every one of us is now obliged to join together.
To halt the spread of this disease.
To protect our NHS and to save many many thousands of lives.
And I know that as they have in the past so many times.
The people of this country will rise to that challenge.
And we will come through it stronger than ever.
We will beat the coronavirus and we will beat it together.
And therefore I urge you at this moment of national emergency to stay at
home, protect our NHS and save lives.
Thank you.
Published 23 March 2020

Wow!

In a few days, I will edit this. I will read through these notes and type them out. I know I will be shocked, again, even though I saw the speech live on television.

I sent messages to family and friends, and posted on social media. I told people to message me if they needed to.

24th March.

The first day of 'lockdown'. It is a slight misnomer, seeing as we are allowed to leave our home for certain reasons. I have accepted the speech from the Prime Minister, extreme as it was, without hesitation. I suppose I am open to this national emergency now, so that which I considered extraordinary a few weeks ago isn't any longer.

I'll include an addition here, not present in the Kindle version. I have authored a few dystopian novels over the years. I am also terrified, TERRIFIED, of ending up in hospital, in intensive care, like the poor souls I see on the television. I wonder if that is why I accepted the rules and guidelines?

Can my imagination 'see' a potential future, as I would see a plot line for a novel?

I worked hard today, and the children settled in with their new, relaxed routine. Some work, some play, some exercise in the garden.

I telephoned my mum a couple of times during the day. She's okay, still laughing and making jokes, but the isolation part of self isolation will annoy and frustrate her the most. Jasmine is visiting almost every night after work, so that's great for lifting the spirit.

Apart from a slight show of frustration from Sawyer, and some rambling questions and concerns from Leon, today was great. I can't really use my old values. JANUARY AND FEBRUARY values. Values from a couple of weeks ago. Unbelievable!

Great news in the family as well, but it's a secret. Haha!

25th March.

Can you guess what the date is today? I'll tell you. It's the 26th of March. I have caught up with my own notes. I'm writing one day behind, so I have some breathing space, and a relaxed schedule for the next week. Perfect timing as well, if you look at it, because the ending is so close.

Mum went out to the shops for us, and we also need to try and find a few items for my mum. It's impossible to know, or even imagine, what the shelves will look like out there at the moment. We can only do our best. You have to remember, though, the staff at supermarkets are working around the clock to replenish stock. Delivery drivers as well, and every other member of the supply chain. If I could, I'd buy them all a drink.

We managed to buy almost every item on my mum's list, so I will drop it off later today. My exercise today will comprise of walking four miles through the streets, minimum! Haha!

On a serious note, I will find the journey interesting. I will take many observations of the changed world, and such observations will no doubt fascinate me and my mind. I was speaking to a few author friends recently, and I joked about how many virus, post apocalyptic, or dystopian books will appear on the shelves, or be released in a year. Personally, I won't write any. I am too busy with this, and many others already planned.

I will work today, although I am unsure of when, for how long, and which areas of the business to focus on. I do know I will watch the BBC news as much as possible.

A lot of other countries have initiated full lockdowns, or partial lockdowns, like the UK. The number of infected people is rising daily, and I don't need a degree in epidemiology to know how terrifying the published data is. I am, however, so glad to see results from China, though, and other parts of the world. Many countries have been in isolation for six weeks, possibly longer, possibly shorter. The virus has been brought under control because of the measures, though, so there is hope for us all in this time of panic, confusion, and complete disbelief.

I arrived back from my mum's by mid-afternoon. Yes, there were people in the streets, cars on the road, workers in certain shops, the permitted ones. I bought some paracetamol and it made me smile. Has it come to that? I smile when I find headache tablets? How the world has changed in such a short amount of time.

I spoke to a friend on social media. She's expecting her first child in July, and is terrified. I can't imagine the normal emotions and feelings of a pregnancy added to by the world locked in their homes because of a virus.

The tests are arriving, in all their different forms. Screening and antibody kits, that's what we keep hearing about. The spokesperson at the press conference said they will check those in hospital, then ALL THE REST are for NHS STAFF, and I AM GLAD! If there are any who deserve it more, I can't think of them.

As I was walking home, I thought a lot about Leon. As you all know, he is due counselling for anxiety issues. I mean, the January publication featured this as a predominant topic. That whole part of our lives seems so distant now. Not forgotten, but ... deferred? Is that the term I'm searching for? It has less urgency, less focus, and less residual stress for everyone involved.

I don't want to presume the thoughts inside Leon's mind, however, does he still worry? Is any of that still present and relevant?

One day, whenever it arrives, Leon will still need to try and return to school. None of this has disappeared, none of the need for him to face the anxieties. During the coronavirus crisis, our attempts to push him, to educate, to overcome, plus the professional help as well we are still waiting to hear about, might not be as consistent. We could reach a new school year in September, or later in the year, and nothing will have changed. All the hours, days, weeks, and months we have already put in could also have been a waste of time. We will all have to start again, from the beginning.

Mum set fire to some of the dinner! Well, the oven did. We saved it, but she can have some serious times in our kitchen, and they usually involve burning herself. It's one of our oldest family memes.

Last week, children were still in school. Last week, we were allowed out, as long as we obeyed hygiene advice. I will not let my imagination run wild, I will not, however, what will I type a week from now?

The government press conference tonight focused on testing for the virus. It is an important topic and always brought up by journalists. Plus, the 405,000 volunteers. Yes, you read that correctly. 405,000 volunteers ... in twenty-four hours. Sometimes, humanity shines so bright, it is seen by all. I might join the telephone staff.

I have had to remind myself what day it is, and too often. I usually reserve that special kind of confusion for when the children are on their school summer holiday. I suppose this is a version of that, simply extended?

Hugo has spoken to a couple of his school friends, so there is some social interaction, and it is so important at the moment. That will be a side effect to all this as well. The sudden loss of our usual routine. In a way, having a large family will benefit us in that respect. Will it also cause arguments, stress, and tension between us we haven't foreseen yet? Probably.

I'll end today with this. I hope you are well, staying safe, looking after yourself, and those who need you as well.

26th March.

Work! Get to work! Get those edits open. Type like you have never typed before!

Yeah. My boss, me, is a total jerk … sometimes. Winky face.

There are bouts of frustration among the children, and we understand it, even though they have access to the garden. We will also solve any instances in a calm and thoughtful manner. They are stuck indoors, thrown into a worldwide pandemic, ordered to leave school, and deal with new worries. It is SO DIFFICULT for young minds to grasp this.

I have relatives in Scotland, so I also try to watch Nicola Sturgeon speak daily. She also impresses me. Her demeanour is perfect for the current situation, I believe. A rousing determination, weaved with a true care for her country.

I mentioned a few lines ago about the bouts of frustration, and it can be called many names. Cabin fever. Stir crazy. Yeah, get ready for more of that in the following weeks and months. Wow. I can't wait. Sarcasm alert.

Mum made some decorations for the children in our block of flats. They can be painted, or decorated, then hung up in their homes. The news keeps reminding everyone, the world over, about mental health being important during the isolation periods, so fun for the children, *any children*, is paramount.

We all went in the garden for fresh air, fun, and family time. We're sharing the space with the neighbours who also have children. Even before all this, we've used the garden well over the years. Parties, birthdays, chats over tea, chats over beer, chats while all the children play together, paddling pools on summer days, and snowball fights.

The Chancellor of the Exchequer, Rishi Sunak. I do not envy his position right now. He is trying to help EVERYONE. EVERYONE IN THE UK. Once again, I find myself impressed. At this point, I must also show my admiration for the scientific community behind all this. Not only in the UK either, but worldwide. I am a science enthusiast. I love science. I love the mystery, the laws, the cogs turning our world, some of which are yet to be fully understood.

I spoke to my mum, as did Jacob. He always puts the phone handset next to his ear and has a ranted conversation. It makes my mum laugh every single time.

Okay, there is a movie on television tonight. Well, when I made these notes it was printed in the newspaper. Contagion.
Why they are showing it I do not understand. It is literally a mirror for the current situation of the world and the coronavirus pandemic. It is not a great idea in my honest opinion. There's bad timing, then there's BAD TIMING.

Today saw a death total of 103 in the UK. That is the highest we have ever seen, and quite a significant increase in comparison to previous days. I know the numbers and data aren't always as straightforward as they seem, but we have already been warned about increasing fatalities, and reaching the first 'peak' of cases. The scientists and politicians said, almost from day one, that high numbers of deaths were expected. I fear seeing the news two weeks from now. I think I have already said that, but, if so, it needs to be restated.

#ClapforNHS. #Clapforourcarers. It happened at eight o'clock this evening, and IT WAS AMAZING! I hope they do realise how much every single person feels about their commitment, caring nature, and strength.

27th March.

I had to go shopping. We needed food for the next few days to cover the family needs. As far as I remember, I managed to buy nearly everything on our list. Yes, the shelves were still empty, but the supermarket had a policy in place. They were only letting in a couple of shoppers at a time, and keeping the numbers inside to a minimum. At a guess, I would say it was close to fifty people.

My mum is bored indoors. In all honesty, she doesn't go out a lot when the world is normal. It's the fact the restrictions are now in place, it feels as if *something* has been taken away from her. You don't miss something until it's gone, right?

Okay, BREAKING NEWS! The Prime Minister, Boris Johnson, has tested positive for the coronavirus! I'm shocked. He posted a video on Twitter, explaining his symptoms and decision. As far as anyone could tell, he was in great spirits, and his determination hasn't wavered. The mild cases of this virus are said to be very similar to a flu, and, thankfully, the Prime Minister stated he feels well apart from a couple of symptoms.

Wait. Wait! More BREAKING NEWS! Another member of the government has gone into self isolation. Matt Hancock, the Secretary of State for Health and Social Care.

No! Even more BREAKING NEWS! Not a third? Seriously? Now one of the scientific faces of this entire situation, Dr. Chris Whitty, has self isolated because of symptoms.

Is it creeping through government now?

The news focused on these three pieces of news today, and I understand that decision.

I am in shock at the new data released by government. 181 deaths. I did hear it is being processed in a different method, or new variables are being included. If that explains the leap, I will be *less* horrified, although not by much.

We had a brief conversation with Leon about his school work, and reassured him as well. So, we are not piling on any pressure, not on any of the children during the isolation and time off school. We have only asked that they keep their minds active.

Apparently, Leon became worried because he looked at some work sent out by his school, and it confused him. He became worried about how his previous time out, due to all the anxiety related issues I have already mentioned in previous weeks and months, had placed him too far behind to ever return to a 'current' level.

We enjoyed our daily garden time with the children. Jacob is loving it out there. He runs, he grabs leaves, he chases his brothers, he kicks footballs.

My notes say, 'Some frustration. Some unnecessary arguments. All sorted, thankfully.' I don't remember why.

I'll add a quick addition here, as I am on the subject. We understand the world is different. We are not going to change the basic, fundamental rules we follow here, but we will also show understanding. Our own ethos has to change, simply because the world has forced it to do so. We can't become angry at the children when their frustrations show through, or trivial angers rise because they are with each other for every minute of the day. In our eyes, we would be punishing for reasons beyond their control.

Only a couple of days remaining until the marketing ends. I do hope the readers enjoy January. I hope parents understand why I truly believe it is important to write these books.

The press conference today contained some … encouraging news. I was going to use the the word 'great', but I don't think it applies at present. I suppose even how I describe positivity has to change?

Yes, they mentioned the Prime Minister, of course, yet they also mentioned new hospitals, new testing facilities, and gave the British public important data explanations. It's small glimmers of hope, that is how you measure positivity now. You have to add up all the small glimmers of hope. It's similar to the shield I have mentioned so many times. Use the good against the bad.

I noticed how worried Mum was. I asked her to stay off the news and social media sites and apps, and she told me how worried she is because of the rise in cases and deaths. News can be intense right now, and it is draining at times to watch all the scenes from around the world, to imagine a couple of weeks in the future.

What did I do?

I …

Erm …

I played 'Sexy and I know it', by LMFAO. Then, I pulled my jeans and boxershorts down, and danced half-naked for a while in front of her. True story. I shall copy and paste from the January introduction.

'Plus dancing. Always shake those hips. Don't question it.'

The children ran out of the room in fits of laughter and embarrassment. Mum laughed at them and smiled. Hey, she laughed because it was funny! No, wait, even that doesn't sound right.

At no point did she laugh at anything she saw. Only because I was super-funny. Yeah, that's better. Haha!

28th March.

How's the Prime Minister? Matt Hancock? Dr Whitty? I shall check the news and find out.

Okay, they're all in good health. Let's carry on with the rest of the day. I expect there will be a lot more to cover.

I do want to make a brief return to the point I made yesterday about 'the shield'. If you read January, you will know how much I used it on a daily basis. Since the coronavirus took over our lives, I haven't mentioned it as much, however, it is PERMANENTLY ON. I watch something terrible on the news, I listen to Jacob laugh. I read an alarming statistic, I make Mum smile. I worry about the pandemic, I chat with Sawyer about his latest computer game victory. I miss my mum and May on their usual Saturday visit, I find Hugo and Leon and tell them a 'Dad' joke.

While I was out at the shops today, *trying* to find the food we need, I thought it looked too normal. There were a lot of people around, and in the town.
As I wrote recently, the Scottish First Minister, Nicola Sturgeon, of who I am a fan, has said on many occasions that if life feels normal, ask yourself if you're doing enough. Life shouldn't feel normal.

We all played in the garden again. The weather isn't amazing and warm, not yet, but the sun is beautiful when it is out. It lifts the spirit.

I spoke to my mum about a local doctor who had died from the coronavirus. She knew him. It makes the entire pandemic more ... personal.

The government figures came in today, and there has been a terrifying rise in the numbers of infected and, sadly, those who have died, over the past few days.

Two hundred and sixty in twenty-four hours.
260.

I won't stop watching the news or press conferences, despite a part of me wanting to hide away from it all. We were warned of this eventuality from the beginning. We were told of the tragedy to come, however, it still doesn't prepare you for when it arrives.

Another member of government, Alister Jack, has placed himself in self isolation. People are concerned, and rightly so, about the virus working through parliament.

We ended the day with FaceTime fun. A joint call with four of the family members, plus our children making appearances. The animal filters made Jacob laugh! Haha!

I woke up during the night, but only for about half an hour. Leon was in the front room, so I had a quick chat with him. He was having trouble falling asleep, so he turned to his trustworthy Youtube to entertain him.

Here's a story to make you all laugh. While I was with Leon, I heard a few scratches near me. If I had to guess, it was in the armchair I was sitting on. We have had a mouse in here before, so, possibly, it was under my arse!

29th March.

Summertime begins here in the UK today. Whatever. It's cold, grey, and we're locked in.

The promotion for the January book ended, so I will keep an eye on the subsequent data. Even in the literary world, statistics help.

A letter is being sent to every household from the Prime Minister. It was on the BBC news website, so I will copy it out exactly.

The Prime Minister

I am writing to you to update you on the steps we are taking to combat coronavirus.
In just a few short weeks, everyday life in this country has changed dramatically. We all feel the profound impact of coronavirus not just on ourselves, but on our loved ones and our communities.
I understand completely the difficulties this disruption has caused to your lives, businesses and jobs. But the action we have taken is absolutely necessary, for one very simple reason.

If too many people become seriously unwell at one time, the NHS will be unable to cope. This will cost lives. We must slow the spread of the disease, and reduce the number of people needing hospital treatment in order to save as many lives as possible.

*That is why we are giving one simple instruction - you **must** stay at home.*

You should not meet friends or relatives who do not live in your home. You may only leave your home for very limited purposes, such as buying food and medicine, exercising once a day and seeking medical attention. You can travel to and from work but should work from home if you can.

When you do leave your home, you should ensure, wherever possible, that you are two metres apart from anyone outside of your household.

These rules must be observed. So, if people break the rules, the police will issue fines and disperse gatherings.

I know many of you will be deeply worried about the financial impact on you and your family. The Government will do whatever it takes to help you make ends meet and put food on the table.

The enclosed leaflet sets out more detail about the support available and the rules you need to follow. You can also find the latest advice at gov.uk/coronavirus

From the start, we have sought to put in the right measures at the right time. We will not hesitate to go further if that is what the scientific and medical advice tells us we must do.

It's important for me to level with you - we know things will get worse before they get better. But we are making the right preparations, and the more we all follow the rules, the fewer lives will be lost and the sooner life can return to normal.

I want to thank everyone who is working flat out to beat the virus, in particular the staff in our fantastic NHS and care sector across England, Scotland, Wales and Northern Ireland. It has been truly inspirational to see our doctors, nurses and other carers rise magnificently to the needs of the hour.

Thousands of retired doctors and nurses are returning to the NHS - and hundreds of thousands of citizens are volunteering to help the most vulnerable. It is with that great British spirit that we will beat coronavirus and we will beat it together.

That is why, at this moment of national emergency, I urge you, please, to **stay at home, protect the NHS and save lives.**

'We know things will get worse before they get better.'
Nervous face. Scared face. Horrified face.

Mental health is one of the most important aspects for us, as parents, through the coming weeks and months. I've had a few moments already when it is difficult to stand in front of this enormous, yet completely invisible, monster. I have enough work to keep me occupied for the next five to ten years, plus family and friends, and many creative areas of the business. Despite all that, I can still find myself trapped in a moment. Do you know what I do, quite a lot? I use the breathing exercise that is available on many smartwatches.

BBC news showed the new local hubs in action. Allow me a moment to explain. An initiative has been created to help 1.5 million vulnerable people in the UK. If they need food, or medicine, while isolating, they are required to contact their hub for assistance. I saw the bags full of food and essentials being loaded onto vans. The system works!

So far, it has been a relaxed day. I watched the news, worked, and spent some creative time with Jacob, Mum, and Leon.

I want to make a brief note about the self isolation measures, especially from the view of the children.

It has been a week since the Prime Minister spoke to the country. In that week, I have been impressed and so very proud of my family. The children could so easily have succumbed to boredom, anger, fear, or any other negative emotions. Apart from a few moments, understandable ones, they have acted remarkably.

That reminds me. I spoke to Leon about school. How does he feel now? I thought.

In all honesty, we believed he would be more nervous about the coronavirus pandemic, but he has, so far, handled it in a very mature way. We hope he is proud? We told him he should be.

More work from the government behind the scenes, yet no sign of the Prime Minister. He has posted videos on social media, and spoken about his pride in the nation.

The medical officers, scientists, and higher echelons of NHS management have been vocal this week. Blunt. Truthful. Honest without hesitation. Thousands WILL DIE. TENS OF THOUSANDS WILL DIE.

That is seen as an expected outcome. What is happening in the world? Many would say a nightmare. It is collective, and we all want to wake up. Sadly, they informed us of 209 recorded deaths in the past twenty four hours. 1,228 total deaths in the UK.

To try and end the night on a much lighter note, I may or may not have pulled my jeans and boxershorts down again. I'll let you decide which. It may or may not become a regular part of our isolation days. Haha!

We still have to finish the excellent Mr. Mercedes, but we're trying Castle Rock tonight, to see if we enjoy it.

It's Monday tomorrow. I hope it's Monday. My mind tells me it will be. That means … wait for it … wait for it … I shall release the second part of this series in about a week! Oh, yeah! Awesome! Shall I dance? Yeah, I probably will. I need all the positive thoughts at the moment.

30th March.

Monday morning. The beginning of a new week. I don't feel positive. I will watch the news all day, as is now usual, however, I will do it with a sense of dread, sadness, and foreboding. There have been deaths and cases here, where I live, in the local hospital.

I was going to predict some numbers earlier. Then, I told myself not to. It would be too horrific, too terrifying.

There were many positive stories on the news today. They reported with extensive detail and optimism about a recent innovation between science and engineering. Google CPAP - (Continuous Positive Airway Pressure). Worldwide, every aspect of life is coming together. We have a common enemy, a global enemy, and we're all working to defeat it.

Although I didn't feel positive a few hours ago, I have been lifted by the news. Seeing Ruth May smile on television will stick in my mind forever. Ruth is the Chief Nursing Officer for the NHS. She has been interviewed many times since the pandemic began, on various topics. Today, she stood inside the new Nightingale Hospital in London, smiling, and she clapped and cheered all the staff inside.

I believe the world will be more altruistic once we have battled through the virus. All the humanitarian acts of kindness, all the support, all the community strength, they will remain with people. I try to live an altruistic life, and it can be so rewarding, even addictive. Humanity will remember how it felt to help others, how it felt to change the life of someone with even a moment of thought and care.

I worked. I worked some more. I tried not to become too embroiled with the news, although it is difficult.

Sawyer is not responding well to the lockdown measures. He wants his freedom, and he wants to be allowed to live his life. Of course, there is no point getting angry or frustrated with us, because these aren't our rules.
We will try and arrange something to keep him more active, and less trapped in, yet he wants more than the back garden. Still, sacrifices need to be made, and selfishness can't exist at the present time. Whatever we suggest, it won't be perfect.

The other children enjoyed art time with Mum. We now have hand painted decorations on the light-tree in our front room! Yes we do!

I dropped off some supplies to my sister at work, for our mum. My brother-in-law has just begun a month off of work, due to closure. It isn't classed as an essential business in the government guidelines. It will make shopping for some of the family easier, and also my sister can avoid the use of public transport.

I spoke to a few friends throughout the day, and impressed myself with some of my own creative efforts at work.

It is now four o'clock in the morning, on the 31st of March. Yes, yet again, I woke up. I think I am going to introduce a fitness plan into my day. Usually, I have daily life as my exercise. I go on the school drop off, pick up, visits to town, visits to see my mum, and everything else that is 'usual'. I already have a stretching routine, and I carry it out two or three times a week. Perhaps, if I introduce a few other exercises, I will sleep better through the night?

31st March.

I didn't take any notes. I didn't take any notes?

Okay, it was only yesterday, so I am sure my memory will manage. I hope.

I shopped for as many dinners as possible. I wasn't successful. We will try again tomorrow, or, what I mean is, Mum will try tomorrow. She seems to have more luck and skill than I do when it comes to meals and ingredients.

Our local supermarket had to close for the day! There was a fire in the neighbouring shop and their freezers turned off, plus there was some smoke damage. It is such a shame. Apparently, they had only just received a large delivery of supplies. In the crisis, supermarkets have been low on stock, as I have documented, so to lose an entire delivery was heartbreaking. We bought them a box of chocolates to cheer them up.

Mum is having a 'bad day'. She is down, upset, and the weight of this crisis is piling on. I'm not saying it isn't there for all of us, or any other parent out there, but, we get through. We *all* get through for the children. Today, she couldn't. We gave her group hugs, made her laugh, and tried to keep a smile on her face.

Our garden time was hilarious. Jacob saw a few bees, and decided to chase them around.

"Where bumblebee gone?"

Brilliant!

As usual, I worked. I'm very close to the end of this book now, so I started to look at formatting and the final stages.

I'll end today, this month, and this book on a sombre note, unfortunately. The death toll rose in a rather drastic fashion overnight. It shocked the whole country.

The press conference was a humbling experience, yet the messages stayed the same. We MUST follow the current rules.

"Hi, Blake."

"Hi, Constance. How are you? Well, I hope?"

"Yes, thank you. I'm fine. You?"

"Yes. Scared, but well."

"Everyone is scared, Blake. Everyone. When have we ever faced such a threat before?"

"Yeah, I thought the same. We have nothing to compare it to. We have no ... reference on *how* to act. Does that make any sense?"

"It does, Blake. It does."

"How ... erm ... are we doing?"

"You are both keeping your loved ones safe, in the best way you possibly can. You are calm, and trying to be 'normal' in your life. Try to remember the sudden nature of all this, Blake. A couple of weeks ago, the children were at school!"

"I know. The world has been changed."

"Perhaps, forever."

"Stay safe, Constance. Go and binge watch Mr. Mercedes, and Castle Rock. You'll love them."

"Look after everyone, Blake. I'll speak to you again in the future. The next book will cover April through to the end of June, but don't wait. Keep in touch."

"You too, Constance."